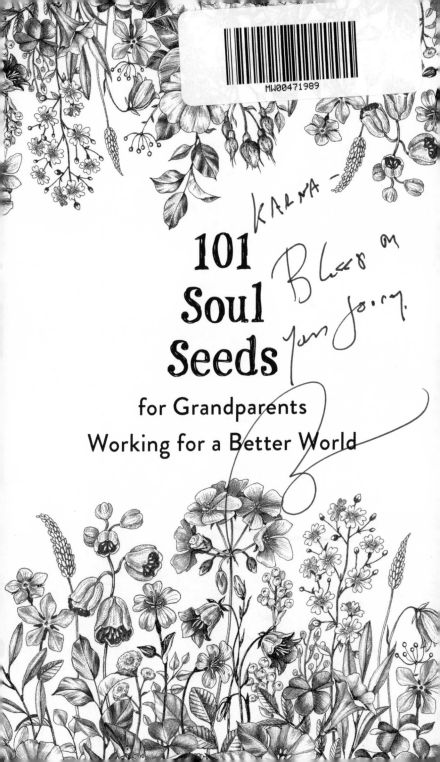

# 101
# Soul
# Seeds

## for Grandparents

## Working for a Better World

*KARNA —*

*Bless on*

*Your journey.*

ANAMCHARA
BOOKS

ANAMCHARA BOOKS
Vestal, New York 13850
www.AnamcharaBooks.com

Paperback ISBN: 978-1-62524-782-7
Ebook ISBN: 978-1-62524-783-4

Cover design and interior layout by Micaela Grace.
Page border drawing by Valiva (Dreamstime.com).

# 101 Soul Seeds

## for Grandparents
## Working for a Better World

BRUCE G. EPPERLY

# Words for
# the Adventure

Grandparenting is a holy adventure. We survived parenting, and looking back, we recognize our virtues as well as our imperfections, often seeing both mirrored in our children's lives. We sought to love and teach our children well, as the song says, so that they might have adventures of their own. Like us, they may fall in love, find a life companion, and raise a family. While we never resign as parents, sometime in midlife we may get a new title: "Grandparent," "Grandpa," "Grandma," "Mama," "Papa"—or "Gabby," as my grandchildren call me.

Last Christmas, my grandchildren gave me a coffee cup with the inscription, "Only the best dads get promoted to Grandpa!" I pray that these words are true as I shoulder two roles in life—father and grandfather.

Grandparenting is truly a holy adventure, seeing and bringing forth the holiness, the inner divinity, of our grandchildren. Showing them in their uniqueness that they are not only our beloved grandchildren but God's beloved children, infinite in worth and possibility.

Grandparenting is constant learning, gaining self-awareness and growing as we interact once again with a younger generation, "bone of my bone and flesh of my flesh." Grandparents are teachers, but our grandchildren are also our teachers, not just as we review new approaches to math, history, and science with them, but as we respond to their unique questions and gifts. Grandparenting challenges us to do our inner work of forgiveness and self-affirmation, letting go of the past and opening to the future, based on decades of life experience. Out of inner work may emerge outer commitments to justice and Earth care.

Grandparenting is an invitation to storytelling. To reviewing our lives and sharing stories that heal, inspire, and reveal our solidarity with our grandchildren. Letting them know that we shared—and may still share—their fears and anxieties but also their courage and compassion.

Grandparenting is global as well as intimate, taking us beyond our relationships with grandchildren to care for children everywhere. The love we have for our grandchildren carries us beyond individual self-interest to care for our immediate family and then to care for this good and precarious Earth. In this time of global climate change, we must look beyond our generation to the wellbeing of our grandchildren's grandchildren.

Grandparenting is prophetic as we ask ourselves, "What kind of world do we want our grandchildren to live in and inherit from us?" and then realize that the injustices of our world have robbed millions of children of the possibility of a happy childhood. What kind of world do we hope for them and what will we do about it? Prophetic grandparenting challenges us to love other people's grandchildren as well as our own, and our love may mean tutoring or leading a scout group. It may mean collecting food for vulnerable families. It also means being part of a grandparents' movement toward preserving the environment; supporting human rights; protecting school children from gun violence; honoring racial, ethnic, and sexual diversity; and promoting justice and equality in the Halls of Congress, local government, and corporate activities.

Grandparenting came naturally to me. I love my two grandchildren and am fortunate to be part of their daily lives. In the Covid season, we homeschooled the boys and created a healthy and safe environment every weekday for six months. My wife Kate and I were weary but also realized Covid-time is not lost time but the time of our lives to be lived fully and lovingly. To provide security, counsel, and affirmation for two growing boys. To create intimate connections and positive memories that will last a lifetime.

This book is an invitation to consider your own grandparenting as a spiritual and ethical vocation or, if you are not yet a grandparent, to catch a glimpse of wonderful possibilities for grandparenting. I don't claim perfection as a grandparent. I am still a pilgrim step-by-step journeying toward far horizons of love. I hope that my words add zest and joy, and perhaps a guidepost for your grandparenting. You will find politics, though not partisanship and polarization, as well as spirituality in this book because the personal is political. Authentic spirituality is earthly good as well as heavenly minded and our prayers may lead to protest as we seek to create a just and healthy world for all grandchildren.

I dedicate this book to my own grandchildren Jack and James and to grandchildren everywhere. May the streets and byways be filled with laughter, may love abound across our planet and imaginations soar, and may all of God's creatures find happiness.

—Bruce Epperly
*All Saints (November 1) 2020*

# 1.

And Jesus took the young children up in his arms, laid his hands on them, and blessed them.

—MARK 10:16, AUTHOR'S PARAPHRASE

In a world in which children were disposable and had little social value, Jesus blessed the children. Children's lives mattered to the Healer from Nazareth. As grandparents, our calling is to be like Jesus—to bless our grandchildren by providing them with love, attention, guidance, and care. Our vocation is to be guideposts to the future for our grandchildren, helping them navi-

gate their way through the moral and spiritual complexities of the twenty-first century.

But our children don't live in isolation. Our responsibility as grandparents is to be diligent in creating a healthy future for our grandchildren and for children we will never meet by ensuring that the economic, ecological, and social environment promotes the well-being of all children even to "infinity and beyond," as Buzz Lightyear from *Toy Story* proclaims. Let us be guideposts and protectors of children, blessing them by bringing beauty to this good Earth.

**Jesus loved the children of the world. Let us love our grandchildren with passion and care. Let our love be a circle beginning with our grandchildren and embracing all the children of this good Earth!**

# 2.

Jesus said, "Truly I tell you,
unless you change and become like children,
you will never enter the kingdom of heaven."

—MATTHEW 18:3

The saying goes, "It's never too late to have a happy childhood." Many of us have dreamed of becoming grandparents. We sought to be mentors for future generations. We may want to heal the wounds of our own childhoods and parenting. But in mentoring, we must mirror our grandchildren. We must embrace a "second childhood." Not senility or irresponsibility but holy playfulness

that builds upon the adventures of our childhood and heals the wounds of our inner child.

It has been said that "angels fly because they take themselves lightly." We can be part of God's realm of Shalom—a realm of justice, laughter, exuberance, wonder, and playfulness. We can be "happy warriors," youthful in spirit and serious in purpose in bringing justice, beauty, and healing to our planet. The realm of God is found in awakening to the wonders of our lives and joyfully joining God in the dance of creativity and love.

Holy One, give me childlike wonder, clear-eyed compassion, justice-seeking action, and holy playfulness. Let the healthy child come forth from me to bless the children around me, bringing joy and healing to their lives and this glorious planet.

# 3.

You are a child of the universe,
no less than the trees and stars.
You have a right to be here.

—MAX EHRMANN, "DESIDERATA"

These lines remind me that I am part of something much larger than myself. Our Creator's circle of love embraces me and it also embraces the universe. I am part of the ebb and flow of that loving creativity. With all my fears and doubts, I belong here, I am the universe's beloved child, and so is everyone else.

I claim this same identity as a child of star stuff and Divine love for my grandchildren. They are children of the universe and they have a right to be here! I claim my role as a mentor and sage and a fellow child, who speaks for justice and the voiceless creatures of our planet and still has time for playing. I can let go of my agenda so that I don't miss the opportunities to behold a wild turkey in the front yard, bright stars before sunrise, and the faces of my grandchildren. I can let the energies of love that brought forth the universe flow through me, enlivening and enlightening, and encouraging beauty in others.

Loving One, may I live globally and act locally. Let me rejoice in awakening each morning to another day of love. Let me live fully, open to the "glow flow" of Divine creativity, living joyfully, gratefully, and lovingly each moment of the day.

# 4.

Your children are not your children.
They are the sons and daughters
of life's longing for itself.

## —KAHLIL GIBRAN

A s a grandparent of two young boys, I am learning that graceful grandparenting means letting go of my vision for them and awakening to
God's movements in their gifts and talents. Sure,
I need to remind them to do their homework, pick
up their clothes, and treat themselves and others with respect—but I also need to give them
spiritual space, all while guiding them with the
example of my own life and words of wisdom that

I impart, providing resources to promote their adventures and then stepping back for them to learn their gifts and explore new routes, many of which I will never travel.

I realize that we are people of privilege who have the resources of time, talent, and treasure, as well as race, to explore freely. I yearn for all children to be able to live out their dreams. Still, in my own little personal world, my calling is to create a playground of love, creativity, adventure, and security within which my grandchildren can venture forth, experimenting with the persons they will become, knowing my love will companion them each step of the way.

Spirit of Transformation and Glory, help me find the balance between caring and controlling, guiding and letting go, and teaching and learning.

# 5.

Teach your children . . .

## —CROSBY, STILLS, NASH, AND YOUNG

As grandparents, we are teachers, mining the wisdom of decades of experience and wise learning. We want to teach our children well—by words, example, faith, and courage, helping our grandchildren live well, love well, learn well, and age well. We are the magi of our time, and we teach by listening and learning, as well as sharing. We teach by growing and embracing new ideas and ways of doing things.

Our children may also be our teachers, welcoming us into the digital world and social media, showing us video games for recreation, and inviting us to share their fantasies. Our children may also teach us to care again—as Greta Thunberg challenges our complacency about climate change or the Parkland kids educate us on gun violence.

Yes, teach your children well and let your teaching be informed by that which you learn from them in the dance of generational love.

Holy One, help me teach by the example of my daily life and commitments. Let me learn what's important through my grandchildren's eyes and let us grow together to bring healing to the world.

# 6.

Whole as an uncarved block of wood.

—TAO TE CHING

Life is too complicated for many of us. We are always on the go, filled with projects and things to do. In such moments, we need to pause awhile, be still, and rediscover the "uncarved block," the "hidden wholeness" at the depths of life.

Covid has taught many of us what is important. We have simplified our lives, focusing on family, deepening friendships on Zoom, email, and phone conversations, along with safely dis-

tant strolls and committing ourselves to generosity in providing resources for food-insecure families. Some of us spend more time listening and less time speaking. The child is the "uncarved block," all hope and possibility, open to novelty and change. In loving our grandchildren, let us awaken to our own uncarved, uncomplicated selves. Let us live in this moment, rejoicing in a smile, delighting in a sunrise, giving thanks for the simplicity of every new breath.

Help me, Spirit, to return to my deep origins in love. Help me let go of the clutter of life, seeking to awaken to beauty, wonder, love, and service.

# 7.

Lord, listen to your children praying.

—KEN MEDEMA

Typos can be illuminating. When I typed singer-songwriter Ken Medema's words, my first rendition was "Lord, listen to your children playing." We need to both play and pray. Playfulness is grounded in the graceful interdependence of life. We are all children of a multibillion-year holy adventure, an evolving process from which each day emerges. Our lives are our gifts, and our children's playfulness is built on the loving creativity of God.

But many children are also praying, with words of fear and pain as well as gratitude. Children who didn't eat last night, children in refugee camps in the Middle East, asylum-seeking children separated from their parents, and children whose parents are out of work and have to go to food pantries for their daily meals. Let us pray for our grandchildren, that their lives might be filled with laughter and learning, and for all the children of the world, that they might have homes, meals, education, health care, and love. Lord, listen to your children praying!

**Loving Spirit, listen to our prayers. Hear our joys and sorrows, our pain and celebration, and sighs too deep for words. Help us be the answer to our grandchildren's and other children's prayers by our generosity and love.**

# 8.

Small is beautiful.

— E.F. SCHUMACHER

Small is beautiful! Small deeds can transform the world! Young persons can be leaders! The world is saved one act at a time. As St. Bonaventure and others affirm, "God is a circle whose center is everywhere and whose circumference is nowhere." That means everyone is at the center of Divine love and inspiration. Everyone can experience Divine inspiration and respond in creative and life-changing ways. Your grandchildren can be leaders, teachers, healers, and spiritual guides, and so can you!

Claim your relationship with the Divine and humbly respond to the challenges you observe in the world. God is acting in you, with you, and through you, making every action a potential life-changer. What are you invited to do today for your personal growth and the well-being of your community and planet? Grandparents can be catalysts in changing the world!

Loving Spirit, awaken me to the wonder and power of what the world considers insignificant. Let me experience my daily life as the playground for Your inspiration and creativity. Let me claim my role as Your beloved companion in healing the world.

# 9.

The kingdom of heaven
is like a mustard seed that . . .
when it has grown it is the greatest of shrubs.

—MATTHEW 13:33

When I was a child, my Sunday school class studied this parable, and I decided to put it to the test. My mother had a box of McCormick mustard seeds and I planted them in her garden. Before I knew it, the mustard seed plants sprung up, adorned with glorious bright yellow buds. After a few weeks, my mother made me cut them down. "They'll take over the garden and spread

to our neighbors' yards," she chided. I've never forgotten that real-life Bible lesson. Small can be contagious and transformative. From small beginnings great possibilities can emerge.

What small thing can you do to transform the world for your grandchildren? Each moment is decisive in adding to or subtracting from the moral arc of history. Your love, your advocacy for immigrants, endangered animals and the environment, and social justice may not seem large, but it can be the tipping point toward God's Shalom. Act small, knowing small acts—like a dripping faucet—done time after time can yield great results.

**Loving Spirit, may my small commitments add up to great changes, tipping the balance from death to life and hate to love.**

# 10.

One of his disciples, Andrew,
Simon Peter's brother,
said to him, "There is a boy here
who has five barley loaves and two fish.
But what are they among so many people?"

—JOHN 6:8-9

These days many of us feel powerless to effect any change in the world. Despite our largesse, the levers of government and the economy dwarf our influence. Still we can, like the young boy with the loaves and fish, share our gifts in solidarity

with others. We can join groups that protect our grandchildren's future, respond to gun violence, and promote black lives. Our small loaves can become a smorgasbord of influence.

We are not alone. We have each other. We have a vision of a just world. Let us pool our loaves and fish to heal the world.

**Spirit of Abundant Life, help me to share my gifts, joining with others to change the world.**

# 11.

No one is too small to make a difference.

—GRETA THUNBERG

In 2018, fifteen-year-old Greta Thunberg started a movement that is changing the world. One Friday, she decided not to go to school to protest the climate crisis. Soon other teenagers decided to skip school as a sign of their concern for the future of our planet and a challenge to their parents and grandparents to use their power responsibly, live more simply, and use less non-renewable energy. She challenged the world's

leaders to become environmentally conscious. Her commitments are an image of hope.

Thunberg asserts: "Every single person counts. Just like every single emission counts. Every single kilo. Everything counts." Each moment is holy and every moment can make a difference in healing the Earth and bringing justice to its peoples.

Holy One, thank You for the opportunity to be Your companion in healing the world. Inspire me to see the importance of every act for myself and for children and grandchildren everywhere.

# 12.

Then I said, "Ah, Lord God!
Truly I do not know how to speak,
for I am only a boy."
But the LORD said to me,
"Do not say, "I am only a boy,"
for you shall go to all to whom I send you,
and you shall speak whatever I command you.
Do not be afraid of them, for I am with you to
deliver you," says the Lord.

—JEREMIAH 1:6–8

Often, we underestimate our impact on the world. The prophet Jeremiah was the young-

est person in his circle. He believed he was unqualified to share God's wisdom. Yet God singled out Jeremiah to challenge the injustice of his time. The example of Jeremiah inspires us to humbly take our place as God's companions in healing the world.

A simple word can change your grandchild's life. A hug can restore a grandchild's spirit. Your solitary voice can shape a family or community. You convey Divine love and healing. Don't be afraid to stand by the oppressed. Don't be afraid to speak for other people's children and grand-children. God is with you to inspire and deliver.

Loving Creator, I reach out to others, sharing the good news of Your love, remembering that one word can make a difference and one life can change the world.

# 13.

To see a World in a Grain of Sand
And a Heaven in a Wild Flower
Hold Infinity in the palm of your hand
And Eternity in an hour.

## —WILLIAM BLAKE

Have you ever heard the word "panentheism"? It's an odd theological word that means "God in all things and all things in God." Like the word "omnipresence," it suggests that every moment points beyond itself and reflects God's creative love. Everything is connected and permeated by

God's loving wisdom. Although we may not see the holiness of life, it exists as our deepest nature, our "original wholeness," as Thomas Merton notes.

God is present in your life as a grandparent, inspiring and guiding you. All creatures, including your grandchildren, are words of God, revealing the Divine presence for those who have eyes to see and ears to hear. Our grandchildren call us to wake up to wonder. Wake up to beauty. Wake up to revelation. God is in you and with you, energizing and uplifting you.

**Spirit of all creation, You are present in every creature and each moment. Wake me up to wonder, beauty, and love. Let me be transparent to Your love and let that love flow through me to my grandchildren.**

# 14.

Whoever destroys a single soul
shall be considered one
who has destroyed a whole world.
And whoever saves one single soul
is to be considered to be one
who saved a whole world.

—ABRAHAM JOSHUA HESCHEL

The wisdom of Jewish mysticism reminds us that every person matters. Every child matters. The time you spend with your grandchildren is holy time. Your love for them is soul-saving and spirit-transforming. Each moment can bring joy,

healing, and direction to a child's life. Each act can have impact that will outlast your lifetime.

While we will make mistakes as grandparents—we may be impatient at times or focus on our concerns rather than our grandchildren's—we can still be spiritually influential persons in their lives, making an indelible difference that will last a lifetime. Grandparenting invites us to be our best selves, to recognize that in our interactions with our grandchildren we are entertaining angels unawares and helping shape God's beloved children.

Loving Spirit, let me experience the holiness of each moment. Let me rejoice in the wonder of life and the amazing singularity of each grandchild. Let me bring joy to their hearts and wholeness to their lives.

# 15.

Let the beauty we love be what we do.
There are a hundred ways
to kneel and kiss the ground.

—RUMI

There are many ways to be a grandparent. Some grandparents live nearby and pick up their grandchildren, like I do, after school. Others communicate via Zoom and other social media platforms. Some are emotional cheerleaders. Others intellectual guides. Love takes many forms, based on our gifts and the unique gifts and needs of our grandchildren. In our grand-

parenting world, I am the homework and reading grandparent. I pick up the boys after school and often shuttle to sports practice. My wife Kate does artwork with the boys and encourages them to learn basic skills of carpentry and gardening.

I once read some great advice about spiritual growth that I think can be adapted to grandparenting: "Pray as you can, not as you can't." We don't need to emulate others' grandparenting styles but rejoice in our own unique relationships with our grands. There are many ways to pray and many ways to love. But the most important way to grandparent is to love—to love by being there, listening, supporting, and sometimes challenging. That will suffice!

**Loving Spirit, help me embody Your love in my grandparenting, loving each child who is placed in my life.**

# 16.

Now there are varieties of gifts,
but the same Spirit
and there are varieties of services,
but the same Lord;
and there are varieties of activities,
but it is the same God
who activates all of them in everyone.
To each is given the manifestation of the Spirit
for the common good.

**—1 CORINTHIANS 12:4-7**

Although most of the people reading this text are over fifty and some like me are nearly seventy (or beyond), all of us have been given ever-young talents and gifts through the interplay of God's creativity and our own. We find joy in living out our gifts.

God has many visions for your life and if you listen, even now, you will discover where the Divine is calling you at this moment and in the future. In embracing your gifts, you model creativity, joy, and generativity for your grandchildren, and bring something beautiful to God's good Earth.

**Giver of All Good Gifts, for my unique gifts, I thank You. For the opportunity to share my gifts with my grandchildren and the world, I thank You.**

# 17.

I will pour out my Spirit upon all flesh . . .
and your young men shall see visions,
and your old men shall dream dreams.
Even upon . . . both men and women,
in those days I will pour out my Spirit.

—ACTS 2:17–18

On the day of Pentecost, a Jewish harvest holiday fifty days after the Christian Easter, Jesus' first followers were filled with the Holy Spirit. They went out into the streets sharing the good news of God's love for humankind. They also proclaimed the universality of Divine revela-

tion, breaking down the boundaries of rich and poor, male and female, young and old, and powerful and powerless. They described a democracy of revelation in which everyone receives the gift of the Spirit's lively, life-changing love and then shares their gifts with others.

You are part of that democracy of Spirit. God has bestowed wisdom, energy, love, and inspiration upon you, unique to your personality, life experience, and community. Your task is to take time to awaken to your particular vocation—and then share it with your grandchildren and everyone else you encounter.

**Spirit of Gentleness and Inspiration, awaken me to Your movements in my life so that I may follow Your guidance, shaping my choices and my gifts to the world.**

# 18.

I believe that God made me for a purpose.
But He also made me fast,
and when I run, I feel His pleasure.

**—ERIC LIDDELL, *CHARIOTS OF FIRE***

After being reprimanded by his sister for neglecting his preaching responsibilities to focus on competitive running, the Flying Scotsman Eric Liddle asserted that competitive running was his calling, something that gave God pleasure.

Do you ever feel God's pleasure? When does it emerge? When I am in the zone, in the flow, the

energy of love propels me forward creatively and lovingly. Sure, we all have to "pay the rent," that is, do the necessary things in life—put out the trash, gather papers for taxes, mow the lawn. But even these tasks can become holy opportunities for growth if we see them as part of our whole lives and dedicate them to the Divine realm. Your grandchildren will grow in joy and creativity by watching you joyfully share a skill and live out your dreams. God has given you gifts; awaken to God's pleasure by living your dreams.

**Giver of All Good Gifts and Inspiration to Joy and Pleasure, let me open to the gifts of a lifetime and this moment. Let me take time to listen for the calling of the moment and the calling of this season of life.**

# 19.

Don't ask what the world needs.
Ask what makes you come alive, and go do it.
Because what the world needs is people
who have come alive.

## —HOWARD THURMAN

What makes you come alive? What gives you a lilt in your voice and a spring in your step? What wakes you up in the morning? This day is the meeting of yesterday, today, and tomorrow; of time and eternity; of earth and heaven. I wrote this text during the time of protest and pandemic, which many of my friends described as "lost time." In contrast, I believe that this is the time of our

lives. This is the day that God has made, let us rejoice, let us be passionate for life and love and justice. One of the greatest gifts that we grandparents can give to our grandchildren is the gift of passion—something to live for and something we are willing to die for. We must share our dreams and hopes and our passionate involvements whether in our unique talents or political actions or spiritual lives. They have their own passions, but to see a lively and passionate elder gives them direction and purpose to their passions. Come alive on this most glorious and unrepeatable day, and the world will ring with joy and celebration even in times of struggle and challenge.

**Enliven me, O Spirit, to the wonder of this day. Let me seize the day passionately—even if I am gentle and understated—loving life and bringing life and energy to others.**

# 20.

Vocation is the place
where our deep gladness
meets the world's deep need.

## —FREDERICK BUECHNER

We are unique as snowflakes. Our gifts and experiences are unique. Our achievements and failures are unique. Yet we are never alone. The philosopher Alfred North Whitehead says that the whole universe conspires to create each moment of experience. Each moment of our lives touches countless others, directly or indirectly. Joined in the intricate fabric of relatedness, we

can choose to respond to the deep needs of those around us. Our lives are our gifts to others. Our choices shape others.

Listen and look. Experience the needs of your grandchildren, your neighborhood, your nation, and then respond out of your gifts. The inner and outer are one. Your deep gladness can spark healing and wholeness in the world. The world is saved one loving and compassionate act at a time.

**God of All People, let my deep gladness radiate into the world, bringing joy, inspiring hope, and promoting justice.**

# 21.

Listen to your life . . .
and then let your life speak.

**—FREDERICK BUECHNER
AND PARKER PALMER**

I have always appreciated the juxtaposition of the titles of books by two of my favorite authors. "Listen to your life," counsels Frederick Buechner, in all its wonder and uniqueness. Listen to your deep yearnings and the moral and spiritual arc of history flowing through you. Listen to God's whisperings, the sighs too deep for words,

as you interact with your grandchildren. Deep down, Divine wisdom is yours.

Then, as Parker Palmer challenges, "Let your life speak." Let your values come forth in your words and actions. Let your passion for the Earth and its peoples manifest itself in your daily life. For your grandchildren and their children that you'll never meet, do justice, love kindness, and walk humbly with God.

Holy One, let me listen deeply to your stirrings in my life and then boldly and lovingly let my life speak, bringing joy and justice to the world and to those whom my life touches.

# 22.

If the only prayer
you can say in
your entire life is "thank you,"
that will be sufficient.

## —MEISTER ECKHARDT

Gratitude puts everything in perspective. When we are grateful, we acknowledge our place within the graceful interdependence of life. We recognize that we are not fully responsible for our gifts or good fortune. They come from the good Earth; from spiritual teachers who have shaped our values and faith; from educators, parents, and friends; from a stable social structure; from access to resources;

and so much more. For some of us, our gifts have been enhanced by the privilege of race and economics. Yes, we are agents, but no one is entirely the master of their fate or captain of their soul.

Thanksgiving leads to generosity and justice. Recognition of our privileges, often due to nation of origin, race, economics, gender, and family of origin, leads us to reach out to others, confronting structures of injustice that promote violence, poverty, and injustice. Thanksgiving is a lifestyle we can teach our grandchildren, one of joyful affirmation and just action.

**For the beauty of the Earth, I thank You, Artist of Life and Love. For the joy of the senses and all good gifts, I thank You. For the ability to be agents of healing and justice, I give thanks.**

# 23.

Now thank we all our God
with hearts and hands and voices,
who wondrous things hath done,
in whom this world rejoices.

## —MARTIN RINKART

The lyricist of "Now Thank We All Our God," Martin Rinkart, was a Lutheran minister who was called to pastor at Eilenburg, in the German state of Saxony at the beginning of the Thirty Years War. A refuge for political and military fugitives, Eilenburg became a hotspot for deadly pestilence and famine. Rinkart and

family provided shelters for plague victims and refugees. During the height of a severe plague in 1637, Rinkart, the only surviving pastor in Eilenburg, conducted as many as fifty funerals in a day, and four thousand in the course of a year, including that of his wife. His thanksgiving came from trusting God in grief and crisis.

Be inspired by Rinkart's example. Teach your grandchildren to give thanks for the goodness of life, creativity, love, and growth, even in challenging times.

**We thank you, O Spirit, for strength in times of challenge, compassion in times of conflict, and hope in times of uncertainty. Let our gratitude lead to generosity.**

# 24.

I thank You, God,
for the wonder of my being.

—ISABELLA BATES

You are wonderful! Your very existence is amazing! This isn't hype but reality. Think of the millions of processes that occur every moment of your life. Imagine all that is occurring as you read these words, billions of processes going on every second. Imagine all that is occurring as I write these words. I don't have to think about thinking—I think! Ideas come in milliseconds and then miraculously appear on my computer keyboard, from mind to neurons to fingers. Who

knows how? Psalm 139:14 affirms, "I praise You because I am awesomely and wonderfully made."

Today, behold! Wonder, be "radically amazed," as Abraham Joshua Heschel said, and give thanks for being yourself—and then live up the wonder of your being, full of wonder in all that you do, creating beauty, and adding joy to the world, all with your grandchildren watching and learning from you. With my friend from the Shalem Institute for Spiritual Formation, Isabella Bates, we can truly thank God for the wonder of our being.

I thank You, Loving Creator, for the wonder of my being. Senses. Thoughts. Emotions. Relationships. The pure amazement of living this moment. Stitch together the moments of my life in wonder and out of wonder, and let me bring forth the wonder-full life of my grandchildren.

# 25.

I thank you, God,
for the wonder of all being.

—ISABELLA BATES

You are wonderful. But so is this marvelous, dynamic, tragic, and beautiful world. "The whole earth is full of God's glory" (Isaiah 6:3). Radical amazement at life itself is an appropriate response when we behold the heavens or a T-cell in our bodies. In her poem, "The Summer Day," Mary Oliver describes spending the better part of an afternoon transfixed by the magical reality of

a grasshopper going about its business, chewing grass, and hopping from one spot to another.

Be a child of wonder. Live ecstatically, rejoicing in the beauty of the Earth, praising the Divine Artist for all good gifts, and letting life's loving and wonderful energy flow in and through you to the world. And then be sure to show this to your grandchildren!

**Awaken me to wonder, awaken me to beauty, awaken me to love.**

# 26.

Gratitude is wine for the soul.
Get drunk.

—RUMI

Can you imagine being drunk on gratitude, as Sufi mystic Rumi commends? We all need moments of ecstasy, when we are taken out of our small selves and experience the grandeur of the universe and intricate and generous interdependence of life. Gratitude deepens and widens the spirit. It takes us to a higher place, inspires joy, and delight in the simple wonders of life. Such ecstasy is almost more than we can take. Yet, this is our world—of risk and danger, yet amazing in all the gifts that flow from the generous hand of God.

So, leave your adult beverages at home and grab the hands of your grandchildren. Get drunk on Nature's colors, the face of your beloved, a dog racing across the beach, a grandchild at play, a gathering of protesters seeking justice, and the face you see in the mirror. In your ecstatic embrace of life, your grandchildren will find a model for healthy inebriation and hilarious highs, natural and lasting through the years.

Deliver us, O Spirit, from dead spirits. Invite us to be large souls grateful for the amazing, tragic beauty of life. Thankful for each moment. Dazed by praise. Drunk with gratitude. Delighted to share our blessings with all we meet, most especially children, vulnerable adults, and persons left behind.

# 27.

Wow!
Thanks!
Help!

## —ANNE LAMOTT

In these three words, Anne Lamott describes her holistic vision of prayer. Wow! Amazement at seeing a grandchild shooting baskets or racing around the house, a superhero in training. Wow! A night filled with stars and s'mores over the firepit. Thanks! Looking across the living room at my wife sending emails to friends on her computer and being amazed at over four decades

of marriage. Thanks! Waking up with more ideas than I can ever put on paper! Help! My fear of the future of my nation and the machinations of its political leaders. Help! My worries about mortality in this time of pandemic.

Gratitude emerges when we realize that every moment is a call to prayer and every encounter an epiphany. In embracing all of life as an inspiration to prayer, we become prayers ourselves, whose love envelopes our grandchildren and flows gracefully to "infinity and beyond."

**Spirit of Surprising Love, wake us up to the great "wow" of life. Remind us to ask for "help." Inspire us always to say "thanks."**

# 28.

For all that has been—thanks!
For all that shall be—yes!

## —DAG HAMMARSKJOLD

Can you claim your life in its fullness? The tragic beauty and wonder of it all. The star stuff of which you are made. The energy of love that brought forth the universe and still courses through every life. The nobility and the small-mindedness. The courage and the despair. Can you give thanks for failures that inspired personal growth? Can you look back at your challenges, affirming "over and over and over, my soul looks back and wonders how I got over?" as the Spiritual asks.

Can we embrace what will come? Now, that's a difficult one for me. There are so many threats—racial injustice and white nationalism, Covid, global climate change, not to mention our own mortality. Still, we can say "yes"—yes to the universe, yes to our personal responsibility, yes to our ability to make a difference, yes to the giftedness of grandchildren and our vocation to nurture their spirits. Upon this great "yes" the future depends. "For all that shall be—yes!"

**Loving Spirit, thank You for all that has been, for my life in its fullness, and for all that shall be, the adventure that lies ahead. May I be bold and creative, loving and committed to justice. Let my life be one great "yes."**

# 29.

Courage is fear
that has said its prayers.

—DOROTHY BERNARD

The times we live in call for courage. We may especially worry about our grandchildren, these vulnerable young people we love so much. Yet our concerns need not paralyze us. Realistic prayer places our whole lives—fear, anger, impatience, joy, and wonder—in God's hands. In reaching out to God prayerfully, we discover that we are not alone and that we have personal resources

to confront every challenge. Realistic prayer also moves us to action.

Prayer isn't magic, nor will it immediately cause all our challenges to disappear, but prayer connects us with an energy and power greater than our own and joins us with people of goodwill everywhere. Prayer changes things, and most of all, it changes us, giving us the courage and grace to get up every morning, face life's challenges, act despite our anxiety, and do something beautiful for God.

**Remind me, Loving Companion, that You are always near and that when I walk beside You, I can face anything, even my fears, and do what needs to be done to bring love, justice, and healing to my loved ones and the world.**

# 30.

We choose to go to the moon in this decade
and do the other things,
not because they are easy,
but because they are hard, because that goal
will serve to organize and measure
the best of our energies and skills.

**—PRESIDENT JOHN F. KENNEDY**

Remember that morning in July 1969 when Neil Armstrong and Buzz Aldrin stepped onto the moon. Glued to our television sets, with hearts beating fast and adrenaline rushing through our bodies, we experienced what was once believed to be impossible. And yet our nation—and human-

kind—faced the difficult and risked failure to advance the human adventure.

These days, many of us are struggling to do the difficult thing. Confronting injustice, for many of us that's difficult! George Floyd, pleading, "I can't breathe," and Breonna Taylor, killed recklessly in a mistargeted police raid, have challenged our sense of American justice and revealed the harsh realities of white privilege, systemic injustice, and racism. We want to look away. But, for our grandchildren, we must do the difficult work of justice-seeking. We are God's hands, feet, and voices and we need to do the difficult thing of facing our privilege and alienation so that God's moral arc of history might be embodied in our grandchildren's—all grandchildren's—lives.

**Loving Spirit, let me not hide from today's personal and political challenges.**

# 31.

I arise today through the power of the Trinity,
Through faith in the threeness,
Through trust in the oneness,
Of the Maker of Earth,
And the Maker of Heaven.

**—ST. PATRICK'S BREASTPLATE**

St. Patrick was often in trouble. An Irish chieftain's price was on his head. Yet he knew that he would find courage and deliverance if he called upon God.

We can't do it alone. We need power and wisdom greater than our own to face the challenges of our lives and the world around us. The power that created the galaxies, inspired the prophets,

guided wise women and men, energized justice seekers, birthed Jesus, and enlightened Buddha flows through us, inspiring, guiding, encouraging, and empowering. We need this power—and an abundance of patience—to be the wisdom givers and defenders of children everywhere. We need to discover courage and wisdom to face our limits in time, talent, and treasure, and then discover resources, beyond our imaginations to give the next generations foundations for integrity, spirituality, and hope. We need to face our passivity when God says, "You are my companion in healing the Earth." Let us rise, trusting the power of God's energy of love, and do our part to heal the world.

Loving Spirit, wake me up each morning knowing that You have given me the power, patience, and love to meet each challenge and to make each day a legacy of love.

# 32.

Christ behind and before me,
Christ beneath and before me.
Christ with me and in me,
Christ around and about me.

**—ST. PATRICK'S BREASTPLATE**

Celtic spiritual guides practice the encircling prayer (caim). Rotating slowly, creating a circle around themselves physically or in their imagination, they invoke the ever-present loving and protecting power of the Divine. Every step we make takes place in that circle of love. Every encounter we have emerges from God's blessing. Every conflict occurs within God's protective care.

We need circles and spirals of love that begin with us and then embrace our grandchildren and families, communities, nations, and this good Earth. With God surrounding us, we can be faithful and do the difficult things that are necessary to embody the Divine's vision of "earth as it is in heaven." (This is a prayer we can share with our grands: ask them to slowly circle to their right three times, pointer/index finger inscribing a circle, and then say a prayer of protection.)

**Circle of Love surround me, Circle of Protection strengthen me, Circle of Wisdom guide me. Let the Circle within which I dwell spiral forth to embrace everyone I meet and every situation I encounter in the day ahead.**

# 33.

Unless a commitment is made,
there are promises and hopes,
but no plans.

—PETER DRUCKER

When you commit to a cause, spiritual path, or relationship, new energies and possibilities emerge. You may not see the far shore, but next steps will come into focus. When my grandchildren were born, my wife and I made commitments to love and nurture them. At the time, we didn't know it might mean picking them up after

school virtually every day or homeschooling and caregiving for months during the pandemic. But we made a commitment and we followed through. We sacrificed time, talent, and treasure, but the rewards of love and seeing two boys grow in a safe, nurturing, and soul-giving environment is worth any sacrifice we might have made.

Consider where you need to make commitments to your grandchildren and to the world in which they will grow up. God is with you on the journey and will strengthen your commitments and give you courage and insight to go the distance with love.

**Strong Power of Spirit, show me what my calling is today and for the long haul. Keep me committed to the tasks You have planned for me.**

# 34.

Where you go, I will go; where you lodge,
I will lodge; your people shall be my people,
and your God my God.

—RUTH 1:16

Ruth is a courageous immigrant. She travels with her mother-in-law Naomi to a foreign land, as an outsider with few resources. She and her mother-in-law might face homelessness and starvation. If it were twenty-first century United States, she might be placed in a detention center or sent off to certain persecution or death. Yet,

she goes forth facing every risk, guided by her love for her mother-in-law. She makes a commitment and follows through. Without the commitment of this immigrant woman, the great mixed-race King David would not have been born, nor would have Jesus!

When we make a commitment to something greater and longer-lasting than ourselves and our achievements, something new is born in the universe. New life emerges, love increases, and justice takes root. Our lives become the catalysts for the adventures of future generations, simply because we said "yes" and stood by it.

**Spirit of Adventure and Inspiration, guide our steps and strengthen our spirits so that we might make commitments to the greater good and live by them one decision at a time.**

# 35.

We may encounter many defeats,
but we must not be defeated.
It may even be necessary to encounter the defeat
so that we can know who we are.
So that we can see,
"Oh, that happened, and I rose.
I did get knocked down flat
in front of the whole world,
and I rose. I didn't run away;
I rose right where I'd been knocked down."

—MAYA ANGELOU

The measure of a person is found in what happens when a dream dies. What happens when a path is blocked? What happens when our reputation is sullied unjustly and our gifts are undermined?

One of the great gifts we can give our grandchildren is the ability to face adversity and respond to problems and failures that come both from the outside and as a result of their choices. There is a power of resurrection and way-making coursing through our lives, flowing with our thoughts and in our bloodstreams that says, "Get up. Run the race, regardless of the outcome. A way will be made."

**Spirit of Unexpected Energy, give us a persistent spirit that we might go the distance, falling down and getting up, as we shepherd future generations toward their promised lands.**

# 36.

Hope is the thing with feathers
That perches in the soul
And sings the tune without the words
And never stops at all.

—EMILY DICKINSON

These days we need hope. It is reasonable to grieve, lament, and want life to change in times of unexpected crisis. Yet, we need something more. We need hope in the future.

Hope is grounded in the affirmation of possibilities and our ability to effect changes in our world. Hope is not magic nor does it deny the lim-

itations we are experiencing. Hope emerges from a realistic sense of our current situation in light of an open future that can be different from the past. Hope emerges in the call and response of God's vision of possibility and our human creativity. Our grandchildren, especially when they are young, are the repositories of future hope. Our task as grandparents is to be gardeners of hope, feeding these young and hopeful plants with our dreams, aspirations, and commitments, and calling them to have dreams and then make them come true.

In times of chaos, Spirit, when darkness overwhelms and leaders have lost their way, let me cling to a realistic hope and let my hopes challenge me to creative action for my time and for generations to come.

# 37.

We must accept finite disappointment,
but never lose infinite hope.

## —MARTIN LUTHER KING JR.

Life disappoints. Dreams are dashed by harsh realities. Justice is deferred. Leaders hang on to yesterday's world, refusing to hear the chants of freedom. Votes are suppressed, elections may be lost and with them the future of the planet is at stake. Finite disappointment is inevitable. But there is an infinite hope grounded in the vision of a deeper reality, the moral arc of history, which

we can only dimly discern but which can get us up each morning with prayers and protests.

History is not complete. Today is not the sum of the quest for justice. Nor are our achievements final. There is a vast horizon of hope ahead, luring us toward "impossible dreams" of Shalom, which take birth when we join hands with God in healing the world. We are the givers of hope to our grandchildren. Don't give up. Look toward the horizon. Spirit is calling us forward.

**Let me be a giver of hope. Let me proclaim an open future. Let me pray and protest, and give my grandchildren hope in a future with liberty and justice for all.**

# 38.

Faith is the assurance of things hoped for,
the conviction of things unseen.

—HEBREWS 11:1

Some of the most important things in life are unseen. Gentle and quiet, the seed pushes through the moist dirt with the dream of the flower. Invisible and mute, the fertilized egg holds within it the hopes of a newborn and then an adult full of possibility to be a catalyst for global healing. Overwhelming wounds become the soil for compassion, creativity, and self-affirmation. Injustice, disheartening and destructive, inspires

marches in the street and Halls of Congress. Death gives way to resurrection. Unseen love inspires sacrifice that saves not only a neighborhood child but inspires national repentance.

Your love for your grandchildren is sacramental, the visible manifestation of an invisible grace, as holy as communion and baptism. Live into hope, and all creation sings with the promise of what is to come.

**Spirit of Unseen Hope, inspire me to trust the unseen seeds, the growing plant, the restless spirit, and let the horizons of hope give me courage to plant seeds and tend the gardens of tomorrow's dreams.**

# 39.

Never place a period
where God has placed a comma.

## —GRACIE ALLEN

A period is an endpoint. A comma is a "perhaps," an invitation to look more deeply into the current challenge, an opportunity to discern the path ahead. Sometimes we quit too early. Life appears to be going against us. Trouble arises. Opponents emerge. Failure occurs and we want to give up. At such moments, we need to become persons of resilience and possibility. We need to pause, assess things, and look for possibilities amid failures.

Our grandchildren are watching. They see how we face adversity. The notice whether we give up or try one more time. They will notice how we face the realities of aging and death. That comma is the great "perhaps" of hopefulness. The open future. The opportunity to test our resilience and make one more try. The grammar of God is punctuated by commas! Byways that open, and possibilities that emerge. Never place a period where God has placed a comma!

Spirit of Open Futures, fill me with possibilities that take me beyond the dead ends I perceive. Give me a holy imagination fitted to inspire possibilities and the energy to attempt them.

# 40.

Faith, by itself,
if it has no works, is dead.

— JAMES 2:17

Faith is a vision of reality that accepts God's enduring and unconditional love and then goes forth boldly to change the world. Faith trusts that the future is in Divine hands. That God has a vision for our lives and is giving us all the energy we need to be God's heart, hands, and feet in healing the world.

God never gives us a vision without providing the first steps to achieve it. God doesn't do our work for us but provides the resources in

energy and encounters needed to be agents of our personal destinies and champions for the young, vulnerable, and forgotten. God wants us to be "heavenly minded," that is, to have a vision of the long haul and trust our lives to God's eternity. God also challenges us to be "earthly good," to bring God's vision to life in our households and in our nation. Let us be faithful workers, sharing the grace we've received to enrich our grandchildren's lives and bring joy to children everywhere.

Spirit of Action, let my words take shape in acts of lovingkindness and hospitality. Let my faith give life to the weary, love to the lonely, and welcome to the stranger so that the highways and byways be filled with laughter and playfulness.

# 41.

Be a light unto yourself,
take no external refuge.
Hold fast to the truth.

## —GAUTAMA BUDDHA

The great teacher Gautama counseled his followers, "Have faith in yourselves." The path to enlightenment is within each one of us. We are all Buddhas or Christs in the making. We are the change we want to see in the world, as Mahatma Gandhi asserted. We are also the ones we've been waiting for, as June Jordan affirmed of South African women marching for liberation.

Jesus said words similar to those of the Buddha when he challenged his disciples to let their lights shine to give glory to God and hope to the world.

Have faith in yourself. Have faith in your deepest intuitions and holy inclinations. Have faith in your highest aspirations. Have faith that your small gifts multiplied over and over can move the mountains of despair and open a pathway your grandchildren will be able to take into the future.

Let me trust the Divine light within me and teach my grandchildren to do the same. Let me bring it forth, let it shine, and show the path of healing to fellow pilgrims and seekers.

# 42.

Faith is a living,
daring confidence in God's grace.

—MARTIN LUTHER

Faith and courage have their inspiration and foundation in grace. Grace is the loving support and acceptance that comes to us prior to any achievements on our part. Grace comes as a gift without conditions and limitations. Grace comes in terms of unexpected energies, new possibilities, and love that overcomes the negative impact of the past and our own frailties and fallibilities. Grace abounds and then inspires us to be grace givers.

One of the most important vocations of grandparents is to be grace givers to our grandchildren. This doesn't mean settling for bad behavior or half-hearted efforts. Grace means full acceptance of our grandchildren, giving them slack that lowers stress and space that allows them to grow in accordance with their deep passions and God's vision for their lives. Grace flows to our grandchildren and ourselves, healing old wounds, building healthy self-esteem, and helping our grandchildren to discover that no failure is final or an impediment to further adventures.

Loving Spirit, I open to Your grace, accepting and embracing my full humanity in its wondrous imperfection. Let me be a channel of grace wherever I go, my acceptance enabling others to discover their inherent giftedness and beauty.

# 43.

Wonder is the feeling of the philosopher,
and philosophy begins in wonder.

—PLATO

Recently my youngest grandson, age eight,
asked me, "What was God doing before the
Big Bang? Where did God come from?" Despite
a lifetime of philosophical reflection, this is way
above my intellectual paygrade. Augustine once
said, "If you think you know it, it isn't God."

But wonder is at the heart of the faith journey. The songwriter confesses, "Oh Lord my God,
when I in awesome wonder consider all the worlds

your hands have made . . ." Long before the Hubble Telescope, the psalmist asked, "When I look at your heavens, the work of your fingers, the moon and the stars that you have established; what are human beings that you are mindful of them, mortals that you care for them?" (Psalm 8:3–4).

One of the greatest gifts our grandchildren can give us is their questioning, their innocent wonder, their imaginations. Listen to your grandchildren. It is never too late to reclaim wonder and amazement. It is never too late to fall in love with a star and hear God's voice in the wind rustling though the trees, and then let your soul sing out, "How great Thou art!"

**Loving Spirit, restore my sense of wonder. Deliver me from boredom and complacency at the majesty of the heavens or the smile of a loved one.**

# 44.

Never once in my life did I ask God for success
or wisdom or power or fame.
I asked for wonder, and He gave it to me.

**—ABRAHAM JOSHUA HESCHEL**

In his play *Our Town*, Thornton Wilder describes the postmortem adventures of Emily, who joyfully watches her family and friends go about their business on an ordinary day. Her joy turns to sorrow when she realizes how little humans appreciate simply being alive. Upon her return to the spirit world, she asks, "Does anyone ever realize life while they live it . . . every, every minute?"

To which he replies, "No. Saints and poets maybe ... they do some." She exclaims, "Oh, earth, you're too wonderful for anyone to realize you."

Heschel asks for wonder, and God fills him with the amazing grace of human existence in all its tragic beauty. Even when he marched with Martin Luther King Jr. to protest the structural injustice of America, he could affirm, "I felt like my legs were praying." It's never too late to have a wonder-full childhood and keep wonder alive for your grandchildren. Pause, notice, open, and then respond to the wonder of even the most ordinary moment.

**Wake me up, Poet of the Universe, to the simple joy of living—breathing, moving, speaking, loving, playing, living, and dying.**

# 45.

Some men see things as they are and ask why.
I dream of things that never were
and ask why not.

## —ROBERT KENNEDY

The great "why not?" Imagination takes us beyond the limitations of the concrete to adventurous possibilities. Too often we are imprisoned by concrete factuality and fail to see that hidden in the facts are seeds of adventure and innovation. Facts are essential, however. Without facts, faith flounders and we are left adrift ethically

and politically. The denial of facts destroys persons and nations. Robert Kennedy knew about the arms race and Jim Crow laws, but his spirit was restless, seeking the horizons of possibility for a "more perfect union."

Not content with the way things are, our imaginations challenge us to envisage what the world can be like for our grandchildren. Imagination empowers hope, which inspires action and creates pilgrims of possibility whose efforts propel the moral and spiritual arcs of history "on earth as it is in heaven."

**Give me a big imagination, big enough to inspire my actions, lively enough to energize my grandchildren.**

# 46.

Once upon a time, I dreamt I was a butterfly,
fluttering hither and thither,
to all intents and purposes a butterfly. . . .
Now I do not know whether I was then
a man dreaming I was a butterfly,
or whether I am now a butterfly,
dreaming I am a man.

—CHUANG-TZU

I am convicted of my self-imposed limitations when I see one grandchild living in the world of Thor, Harry Potter, and Spider Man and the other seeing himself playing in the World Cup

Soccer Match or the NBA Finals. I am more than I can imagine, and so are they. I am a multitude, as Walt Whitman says.

Within the context of your family and professional responsibilities, you can embody what biblical scholar Walter Brueggemann describes as the "prophetic imagination," entertaining alternatives to our current culture of death and destruction, working to incarnate these in your grandchildren's lives, as well as in the halls of Congress and the world of business. Let your imagination roam, push the boundaries of your known world, and then bring that novelty into daily life.

Spirit of Imaginative Love, let me play with the adventures of ideas and envision the architecture of justice, and then do my part to bring something beautiful into my grandchildren's world.

# 47.

Our goal should be to live life
in radical amazement . . .
get up in the morning and look at the world
in a way that takes nothing for granted.
Everything is phenomenal;
everything is incredible;
never treat life casually.
To be spiritual is to be amazed.

**—ABRAHAM JOSHUA HESCHEL**

Remember Louis Armstrong's song: "And I say to myself what a wonderful world!" That's radical amazement. The amazement of a child

asking why there is something rather than nothing. The amazement at the scales of a pangolin or a whale breaching. The amazement of falling in love and staying in love for decades. The amazement at love willing to sacrifice itself for the well-being of the planet or a cause greater than ourselves

The times call for amazement at this good Earth—and then sacrifice for our grandchildren's world and the generations we'll never meet.

**Open my eyes, Spirit, to the magical, miraculous world around me. Break open and cleanse my senses that I might rejoice in the infinite wonder of this tragic and beautiful planet.**

# 48.

Now to him who by the power at work within us
is able to accomplish abundantly
far more than all we can ask or imagine.

—EPHESIANS 3:20

We live in a world of wonders, pushing the boundaries of our imagination because our world is energized and guided by a wonderful Spirit. God's power is loving power, partnering power, healing power, and relational power. God is not out to get us. God is out to love us, aiming at abundant life for us and all creation. What will you ask for? What will you imagine? Hindu

sages speak of the universe as a manifestation of Divine play and recognize that God's playfulness is also the serious business of world creating. Divine world creation is moving in our lives.

I created nations and drew maps of them as a child. My grandchildren create cities of Legos. No doubt our creativity reflects God's creative power "at work within us," as the Apostle Paul proclaims. Today, like the imaginative and creative child you once were, let Divine artistry and poetry move through you—and encourage this in your grandchildren—so that you might receive more than "we can ask or imagine" for our own joy and the healing of the world.

**Holy One, let me ask for bold blessings and out of my blessings, bless the world.**

# 49.

Alice laughed. "There's no use trying," she said.
"One can't believe impossible things."
"I daresay you haven't
had much practice," said the Queen.
"When I was your age,
I always did it for half-an-hour a day.
Why, sometimes I've believed as many as six
impossible things before breakfast."

–LEWIS CARROLL

Can we believe impossible things? Can we dream of our deepest selves and incarnate beauty and holiness, making each encounter a sacramental offering to a Loving Companion? We must dream big and within the context of our personal and professional commitments, and live big, seeing each day of our lives as a holy adventure. Henry David Thoreau counsels, "If you have built castles in the air, your work need not be lost; that is where they should be. Now put the foundations under them."

Let us listen to our grandchildren's dreams and let them awaken us to our own childhood dreams. Let us protect our grandchildren's dreams so that they will always soar.

Make me big, O Spirit, in imagination, love, and creativity. Give me a vision of a world where all are pilgrims but none are strangers.

# 50.

Peace is every step.

## —THICH NHAT HANH

The quest for peace unites the inner and outer journeys. Without inner peace, there will be conflict in our families and communities. Peace is not merely the absence of conflict, but the positive state of Shalom, of wholeness, that pervades a community and adds to the happiness and fulfillment of children and their families. Vietnamese Buddhist monk and social activist Thich Nhat Hanh believes that we can join inner and outer peace one moment at a time. Peace comes from mindful living as we go about our daily lives. For

Thich Nhat Hanh, peace is as near as our next breath. He counsels a simple breath prayer as an invitation to experience peace regardless of the circumstances of life: "Breathing in, I feel calm. Breathing out, I smile."

Throughout the day, breathe peace. Experience your connection with all creation. Share common breath with your neighbors and grandchildren, and let peace begin with you. (You can teach your grandchildren a simple breath prayer: breathing deeply, feeling calm and energy entering them, and breathing out prayerfully into the world, focusing on particular friends or situations.)

Breathe in me and through me, Holy Breath of Life. Let me experience Your peace, so that I might be a beacon of peace wherever I am.

# 51.

If you want to end the war,
instead of sending guns, send books.
Instead of sending tanks, send pens.
Instead of sending soldiers, send teachers.

—MALALA YOUSAFZAI

Pakistani activist and Noble Prize winner Malala was nearly assassinated in retaliation for her quest for justice. She knows firsthand that peace is not just a word but a way of life that must encompass everything we do from speech to economics. Peace is a matter of priority. Will we choose life and health or death and violence? Will we love

our neighbors as ourselves? Will we sacrifice for the greater good of our families and our planet?

Our grandchildren need us to be justice seekers and peacemakers in our households and communities. They need to see us advocating for the vulnerable and the poor. They need to witness us in action: protesting injustice prayerfully and challenging falsehood with kindness and civility. Let us widen the circle of peace to embrace all creation, in the marketplace, the halls of Congress, the White House, and our own homes. Let peace emerge with every breath and step we take.

**Let me be a peacemaker, O Spirit. Let me hear the cries of the poor and experience the pain of the vulnerable. Let me be a healer of wounds and repairer of relationships. Let me be Your companion in mending the world.**

# 52.

Deep peace of the running wave to you
Deep peace of the flowing air to you
Deep peace of the quiet earth to you
Deep peace of the shining stars to you
Deep peace of the gentle night to you
Deep peace of Christ the light of the world to you
Deep peace of Christ to you.

**—CELTIC BLESSING**

There is a deep peace beneath the storms of life. There is a peace that passes all understanding that undergirds the conflicts of domestic life and

politics. We awaken to this peace and share that peace with others. Peace is not only every step; it is also every breath and every word. Gautama Buddha believed that one of the eight steps to peace was "right speech." Speech that is truthful, kind, compassionate, and joining. Speech that is honest and factual. Speech that calms and heals. Peace that challenges injustice while seeing the holiness of those who perpetrate injustice.

When you say "hello," your words can be a prayer. When you pick up grandchildren after school, your greeting can be a blessing. When you speak the truth, your words can heal and uplift. In times of crisis, truth saves lives and mobilizes a nation. Deep peace can flow through you and bring healing to the planetary challenges we face.

**May deep peace encompass every action I take, every word I say, every thought I have.**

# 53.

Jesus said to them, "Peace be with you.
As the Father has sent me, so I send you."
When he had said this, he breathed on them
and said to them, "Receive the Holy Spirit."

—JOHN 20:21–22

Can you imagine Jesus breathing in you? Can you imagine Jesus giving you spiritual CPR to revive your spirit and energize your whole being? Can you visualize Jesus' breath still flowing through the planet, and entering you with each inhaling? One of my spiritual teachers,

Allan Armstrong Hunter, taught his students the following prayer, "I breathe the Spirit deeply in, and blow it peacefully out again." As we inhale, we can experience the Breath of Life energizing and calming. As we exhale, we can feel our breath bringing peace to our grandchildren, families, and community. God's peace comes with every breath.

Let our lives be filled with peace that inspires peacemaking and justice-seeking, and solidarity with all God's creation, as examples to our grandchildren.

**I breathe your deep peace, dear Breath of Life. Breathe on me, in me, and through me, so that every breath is a prayer and every act brings peace on Earth and goodwill to all.**

# 54.

Peace cannot exist without justice,
justice cannot exist without fairness,
fairness cannot exist without development,
development cannot exist without democracy,
democracy cannot exist without respect
for the identity and worth
of cultures and peoples.

—RIGOBERTA MENCHU

Awarded the Nobel Prize for Peace in 1992, Rigoberta Menchu has sought social justice for the indigenous peoples of Guatemala. She knows that "law and order" is oppressive unless it is joined with the affirmation of diversity, self-

determination, reconciliation, and justice for those whose voices have been silenced. While peace may begin with our individual well-being, it must include structures of justice and equality.

Our grandchildren need to find ways to grow up in a world in which cultural, national, religious, racial, and ethnic diversity is affirmed. Where immigrants are treated with respect and fairness. Where sexual orientation and gender diversity is welcome. Peace can be noisy, embracing the songs and melodies of every culture and joyful play of well-nourished children. All the colors of the rainbow bring peace, each unique, each complementary, each beautiful.

Let me experience the voices of otherness, Spirit. Let the yearnings for freedom, often stifled by political leaders, be my yearnings. Let justice be my calling at home and in the world.

# 55.

Walking 25,000 miles
on foot for peace.

## —PEACE PILGRIM,
## MILDRED LISETTE NORMAN

I met Peace Pilgrim first in the 1970s and then in 1980. After a mystical experience, she gave up a promising career to walk, carrying a simple apron, penniless, and dependent on the kindness of strangers who soon became friends. She believed, with St. Augustine, that "it will be solved in the walking." Like Thich Nhat Hanh,

she believed we find peace one step at a time. She saw holiness in those who taunted her, and she believed that political leaders can be converted to pathways of peace.

Each day we embark on a holy adventure. Each day, even in the middle of challenging times, our steps can bring peace to the world. Our words can soothe the anxious and challenge the complacent. Each step can be an invitation to bringing peace to the Earth. We can save the world one step at a time—and show our grandchildren to do the same.

**Holy One, let me strive for a world in which peace is gained with every step.**

# 56.

Peace is self-control at its widest—
at the width where the "self" has been lost,
and interest has been
transferred to coordinations
wider than personality.

**—ALFRED NORTH WHITEHEAD**

The Christian scriptures describe Jesus as growing "in wisdom and stature and favor with God and humankind." Peace involves a deepening and widening of our spiritual senses. Peaceful people are large-souled people, "fat souls" (to use the term of theologian, pastor, and artist Patricia Adams Farmer), whose interests

go far beyond personal gain to encompass the well-being of the planet. They experience unity with all creation.

My authentic well-being brings healing to the world, and your authentic well-being brings me joy and joy to the world. Peace is the spirit of "ubuntu," the Southern African phrase that affirms, "I am because of you." Our grandchildren, our children, ourselves—we are all in this together. When we live out our unity, we will have peace, and our inner and outer lives will be blessed and bless the world.

Give me a large soul, Heart of the Universe, to feel the pain and joy of creation, to affirm the wondrous pluralism of life and bring peace to every encounter. May my grandchildren see in me an example of a "fat soul."

# 57.

The teleology of the universe
is aimed at the production of beauty.

## —ALFRED NORTH WHITEHEAD

What kind of world do you live in? Is it silent and meaningless? Is it chaotic and disorderly? Is it predetermined, with no room for human agency? Or is it a world inspired by the interplay of purpose, novelty, and free play? There is plenty of randomness in our world, but there is also a movement toward beauty that we can see in the emergence of galaxies, the biodiversity of our planet, and the amazing multiplicity of human culture and experience. Within the movements of

planetary history and evolution is a spiritual and moral arc, aiming at beauty and justice. God is an artist and poet, who constantly seeks to evoke beauty from the world around us and our lives.

Look around. Experience the beauty of the stars above, the flowing stream, crashing waves, soaring eagle, grasshopper chewing a blade of grass, a pangolin feasting on ants, and the amazing uniqueness of a grandchild spinning tales or running across the lawn. With beauty all around us, we live.

Artist of the Universe, we give thanks for the beauty of the heavens and our immune system, a child waking up from a nap and an adult seeking to bring justice to the vulnerable and forgotten. Help us see our own beauty and commit ourselves to adding to the beauty of the Earth, doing something beautiful for You.

# 58.

The great philosophical tradition tells us . . .
that when you confront something beautiful
you should begin to
educate yourself and repair the world. . . .
Beauty comes out to greet us
and prepares us for the other undertakings,
for finding out about truth
and committing ourselves to justice.

—ELAINE SCARRY

Noticing beauty has moral implications. To see beauty inspires reverence and protection. As the philosopher Plato asserts, the obvious beauties of the Earth lead us to experiencing the deeper

beauties of life. Our encounters with beauty may challenge us to explore the ecological foundations of the beauties we experience. The connectedness of life helps us discover what is necessary to preserve beauty. This takes us to the realm of truth and justice. The preservation of beauty, especially in a time of global climate change, requires a commitment to factuality wherever it leads us. Prevarication and denial lead to death and division.

For our grandchildren's sakes, we need to move forward to a new garden of beauty. Beauty inspires us to a politics of empathy and holiness, recognizing and responding to the pain we inflict on the nonhuman world as well as the divinity inherent in all life.

**Let beauty inspire truth and justice. Let my circles of care expand to include not only my grandchildren but all humankind and the nonhuman world as well.**

# 59.

Look at the animals roaming in the forest:
God's spirit dwells in them. . . .
God's spirit is present in plants as well.
The presence of God in all things
makes them beautiful and
if you look with God's eyes,
nothing on earth is ugly.

—PELAGIUS

God is ubiquitous and constantly moving through our world. All creation sings with spirit. All creation embodies Divine creativity. Divine incarnation is not restricted to the stable in Bethlehem but radiates across the universe. Wonder and reverence fill our spirits as we discover our own beauty, as incarnations of God, and the Divine revelation in our grandchildren, and in our human and nonhuman neighbors.

Artist of Creation, cleanse my senses and spirit that I might see beauty in all things and bring it forth by my reverence and love. Give me the wisdom and love to teach this perspective to my grandchildren.

# 60.

Despite everything,
life is full of beauty and meaning.

## — ETTY HILLESUM

Can we proclaim the beauty of life when our world is collapsing? Etty Hillesum knew both beauty and ugliness. She felt the anxiety of the German occupation of her Dutch homeland and the fear of being deported to a concentration camp. She experienced anti-Semitism, and eventually, she was arrested and taken to Auschwitz, where she died before her thirtieth birthday. Despite tragedy, she saw beauty. She experienced

meaning in relationships and generosity to others. She believed that beauty will outlast ugliness and love will survive hate.

There is much to lament these days. There is also a counterforce of beauty that will stand long after the voices of hate and fear have been silenced. Seek beauty everywhere, most especially in the children of the world. Trust the moral and spiritual arcs of history. Act to add to the beauty of this good Earth.

**Let my trust in beauty lead me to speech for the vulnerable, innocent, and voiceless. Let me honor the beauty of my grandchildren— and children everywhere—and ensure by my commitments the love that endures after the voices of hate have been silenced.**

# 61.

God is the poet of the universe
leading it by His vision of truth,
beauty, and goodness.

## —ALFRED NORTH WHITEHEAD

Imagine God as a poet and artist, whose primary goal is to bring truth, beauty, and goodness to our planet. God covers the Earth with beauty and inspires beauty in our souls. The Divine Poet invites us to be poets as well. To create beauty in our relationships. To see our lives as works of art. To make poetry and song from the alphabet of our daily lives.

God challenges us to look at our grandchildren and learn to be young again in order to join God in healing the world. Our beauty adds to God's beauty and flows into the world, energizing, enlivening, and enlightening all creation.

Inspire me, Creative Spirit, with the artistry of creation, and let the artist and poet within me burst forth in beauty and service.

# 62.

Whenever you are creating beauty around you,
you are restoring your own soul.

—ALICE WALKER

We live in a bountiful world. Our generosity expands our spirits. Our commitment to beauty awakens our hearts and minds. Our creativity adds to the beauty of the world. Beauty shared fattens the spirit and expands our impact on others. Beauty is not depleted but finds its energy in the Deeper Beauty of the Divine. God leads us in paths of beauty.

Beside still waters, our souls are restored. An ever-flowing stream of beauty flows through us to creation. That refreshment inspires in us as grandparents the beauty of creativity, wisdom, and service. Energized by the Artist of the Universe, we become artists, repairing a broken world and renewing beauty on this good Earth.

Let me live by Your abundance, O Beautiful Spirit. Let me open to Your ever-flowing stream of creativity. Let it flow through me, colored and shaped by acts of beauty, to nurture and nourish my grandchildren and the entire beauty of creation

# 63.

With beauty before me, may I walk.
With beauty behind me, may I walk.
With beauty above me, may I walk.
With beauty below me, may I walk. . . .
With beauty all around me may I walk.

**—NAVAJO BLESSING WAY**

Indigenous people know tragedy. They have lived through genocide and political disenfranchisement and continue to be at great risk from various negative forces in our society. And yet the Navajo people affirm that life begins in beauty, and as the blessing prayer concludes, "It is finished in beauty."

Beauty is a matter of both perception and actuality. We live in a beautiful world. Beauty is baked into the galaxies, as the Hubble Telescope has revealed. The starry, starry night and the T-cell protecting our lives reveal Divine beauty. May our souls reflect to our grandchildren the holiness of beauty and the beauty of holiness as we walk with beauty all around.

Let my grandchildren walk with beauty all around. Let them walk with love all around. Let them walk with healing all around. May I too begin this day with beauty and tonight, as I fall asleep, may I give thanks for the beauty of life.

# 64.

Only the suffering God
can help.

## —DIETRICH BONHOEFFER

Imprisoned and later executed by the Nazis for resisting Hitler, German Lutheran pastor Dietrich Bonhoeffer describes God as feeling the pain of the world. A distant, apathetic God cannot help us. A God who refuses to feel our pain cannot support us. But an empathetic God who experiences our joy and sorrow can address our needs, providing comfort and challenge.

The philosopher Alfred North Whitehead refers to God as the "fellow sufferer who understands." God's empathy inspires our empathy with our grandchildren, and with the vulnerable and suffering persons in our midst. God's whole-person love inspires us to see "the least of these" as our siblings. When we discover God weeping with our tears, we are inspired to dry the tears of others and be God's companions in transforming pain to joy, and lamentation to celebration.

**Loving Spirit, let me experience Your joy and sorrow, and respond to Your vision of a healed and healthy Earth. May I be sensitive to my grandchildren's sorrows and convey to them Your loving compassion.**

# 65.

For those who want to save their life will lose it,
and those who lose their life for my sake
will save it.

—LUKE 9:24

Spirituality is about expanding the size our interests to include others. When we let go of self-interest and the stranglehold we have on life, new energies pour into us, energizing and reviving and propelling us toward the future. Seeking to save our lives, putting our needs ahead of everyone else's, our world shrinks to the size of the present threat or competitor. Losing our lives and expanding our spirits awakens us to

the world of ubuntu, "I am because of you," and we discover ourselves in a world of friends and neighbors. Letting go of our grip on time, talent, and treasures literally saves our lives to love more fully and broadly.

In sacrificing our agendas for the sake of our grandchildren's well-being, we discover our time, talent, and treasure is restored and multiplied. We learn the wisdom that giving and receiving are united and interdependent in God's calculus and that those who sacrifice for others receive a bounty of heavenly blessings.

**Spirit of All People, let me be emotionally, physically, and financially available to my grandchildren, as well as to all persons in need. Let me discover that giving deepens my soul and energizes my body.**

# 66.

We are all called to be saints. . . .
We might also get used to recognizing the fact
there is some of the saint in all of us.
Inasmuch as we are growing,
putting off the old man and putting on Christ,
there is some of the saint, the holy, right here.

**—DOROTHY DAY**

Every so often my wife chides me in public with the words, "I live with a saint" and I'm not always sure it's a compliment! I always decline the title, but the truth is, I do want to be a saint. In part because I think everyone is called to be

saintly in her or his own way. Everyone is called to grow in wisdom, stature, and love. To expand their sense of neighborhood to embrace the whole Earth. The fact of the matter is that I don't just want to be a Christian saint. I want to be a Buddhist bodhisattva, who prays that all sentient beings find joy and defers Nirvana until all sentient beings are enlightened. I want to be a little Christ who shares Divine love with everyone I meet. Saints are bodhisattvas and bodhisattvas are saints, who simply want to broaden their horizons to be partners in the holy adventure of saving the Earth and its inhabitants. Modeling these objectives show our most sacred values to our grandchildren.

**Let me expand my concerns to embrace my grandchildren, children everywhere, and this good Earth in all its wondrous diversity.**

# 67.

Today it is not merely enough to be a saint,
but we must have the saintliness
demanded by the present moment,
a new saintliness without precedent.

### —SIMONE WEIL

It was once said that we need to have the Bible in one hand and the *New York Times* in the other. Today we would add our social media newsfeeds, Facebook, and Twitter.

Vital spirituality is concrete and dynamic. While it may be heavenly minded, that is, looking beyond the chaos of the present moment, it is also engaged and embedded in the messiness of

history, economics, and politics. The saintliness demanded of the present moment must embrace not only our grandchildren and the rest of our families but range to the ends of the Earth. Today's saints must become healing companions in facing environmental collapse, racial and economic injustice, incivility, and bullying. Saints speak for the silent and protest for the persecuted. Yes, I want to be a saint and a bodhisattva, loving not only my grandchildren deeply but all children, working to heal the world, and trusting God with the outcome.

**Let the saint in me come forth, immersed in the joys and sorrows of the world, in solidarity with all, seeing the Divine Spirit in all, seeking a world in which my grandchildren—and all sentient beings—experience authentic happiness.**

# 68.

What is the fruit of study?
To perceive the word of God
in every plant and insect,
every bird and animal,
and every man and woman.

**—NINIAN'S CATECHISM**

Spiritual study is of little value if it deadens our sense of kinship with all creation. Study is intended to transform our lives, so says Ninian, the fifth-century Celtic saint. The words we read and the meditations of our hearts can change the way we interact with our grandchildren, as well

as how we look at the world. When we perceive God's creative word in all creation, we cultivate reverence for life. We sacrifice our comfort not only our grandchildren but also for the survival of bees and butterflies. We set examples for our grandchildren by limiting our personal and corporate activities to sustainable practices, honoring endangered species. We refrain from behaviors that demean our fellow humans. With the doors of perception cleansed and opened, the wonder of each being bursts forth, and we respond with gratitude, reverence, and praise. We will demonstrate to our grandchildren a new way of living.

Let me see You more clearly, love You more dearly, follow You more clearly as I waken to each new day. (Inspired by Saint Richard of Chichester and *Godspell*.)

# 69.

Let us live simply
so others simply live.

## —ST. ELIZABETH ANN SETON
## AND MAHATMA GANDHI

Attributed to sages from both the East and West, this call to simplicity involves sacrifice of certain pleasures for the greater good of our children and grandchildren. We are encumbered by our possessions, stressed by seeking to hold on to our largesse, and worried about the future. In contrast to our fearful possessiveness, Jesus invited his followers to "consider the lilies" and

trust that if we see God's realm, we will have everything we need.

The times call for spiritual decluttering and economic downsizing. In living with less, we move toward leaving our grandchildren a more sustainable world. We can lessen our carbon footprint and have more resources to respond to our vulnerable human and nonhuman siblings. In letting go, our spirits soar, unencumbered by possessiveness and we will know the simple joy of kinship with all creation.

**Holy One, give us contentment with the simple gifts of life, trusting that when we turn from consumerism and possessiveness, we will turn round right.**

# 70.

God is revealed in a personal and intimate relationship with the world. He does not simply command and expect obedience; He is also affected by what happens in the world, and reacts accordingly. . . . The notion that God can be intimately affected, that He possesses not merely intelligence and will, but also pathos, . . . defines the prophetic consciousness of God.

—ABRAHAM JOSHUA HESCHEL

In his book on the Hebraic prophets, Abraham Joshua Heschel introduces the term of Divine pathos—God's experience of the pain and joy of the world. God is the ultimate empath, the fellow

sufferer who understands us, the intimate companion who rejoices with us. God grieves with a child missing in-person school and sports due to Covid restrictions. God laments the razing of rainforests contributing to global climate change. God feels the suffocation of a young man who cries out, "I can't breathe," and the anger of those who protest racial injustice.

Grandparents are also empaths. We feel the pain and joys of our grandchildren. We dry tears and lift spirits. And we claim our vocation as healers in our families. Our empathy may lead to prophetic protest aimed at healing the soul of our nation and the planet and grandchild.

**Let Your empathy be mine, Heart of the Universe, and let my empathy inspire my grandchildren to care for others and challenge me to move from feeling to acting to heal the planet.**

# 71.

He has told you, O mortal, what is good;
and what does the Lord require of you
but to do justice, and to love kindness,
and to walk humbly with your God?

—MICAH 6:8

God has a personal relationship with every creature. The One Whose Heart is Open to All feels our pain and joy. God hears the cries of the poor intimately. God wants every child to have enough food, shelter, health care, and education to flourish. God wants every child to have the privileges most of our grandchildren have— most especially the ability to have a childhood. Howard Thurman, the African American mystic

who has shaped my spiritual journey, states that one of the greatest evils of poverty and injustice is its dampening of a child's imagination.

We cannot turn away from the realities of racial and economic injustice, evident during the pandemic in the inability of some children to receive meals when schools are closed and the digital divide between those who have and those who lack laptops and internet access. God calls grandparents to be prophetic. To challenge ourselves, our communities, and our governments to care for the vulnerable and side with poor. To walk humbly and to do justice and follow God's way.

Loving Spirit, wake me up to the cries of the poor. Wake me up to the prayers of children. Let me seek justice in Congress, in the town square, and in my relationships.

# 72.

If I am not for myself—who will be?
If I am only for myself—what am I?
If not now—when?

—RABBI HILLEL

Rabbi Hillel, who lived a generation before Jesus, joined advocacy for self with advocacy for others. God calls us to speak up for ourselves; Moses spoke up for his people in bondage. Rosa Parks refused to move to the back of the bus. LGBTQ persons, their parents, and grandparents took to the streets for equal rights. A woman speaks up, reminding a bullying politician of her equality, with the words, "I'm speaking!" Authen-

tic self-love refuses to be silenced. Authentic love for others refuses to accept the silencing of others.

I was proud of my two grandchildren when they drew a Black Lives Matter poster and put it on our front door. I am proud of these boys when they remind me to bring canned goods to the food pantry and help me deliver backpacks filled with school supplies to local schools. By our commitment to justice, our grandchildren learn to be just, most especially to the vulnerable and forgotten. Rabbi Hillel concludes, "If not now—when?" Justice cannot be deferred. We need to be part of the fierce urgency of hope: lives depend on it, children depend on it, our world depends on it.

**Spirit of Restlessness, let me make space for others to speak, recognizing the privileges I have that others lack, and model justice and mercy for my grandchildren.**

# 73.

Justice is what love looks like in public.

—CORNEL WEST

The personal and the political cannot be separated. There is no such thing as "it's just business." Nor can we separate the call to love our neighbor from our political involvement. When businesses or governments harm other people's children, I have learned to feel the pain of parents and grandparents. I pray for those who suffer injustice. I pray that thoughtless business and political leaders experience the pain their decisions are creating. I also find ways to stand with those whose human rights are violated and who

are victims of policies that discriminate based on gender, sexuality, race, and ability. They too are someone's grandchildren.

My grandchildren are at the heart of my life. Their joys are my joys and their sorrows my sorrows. My love for them requires me to love others by my choices in the ballot box and political advocacy. Political involvement may not seem spiritual to some people. But, if God's love took form in a homeless Bethlehem baby, then spirituality must be embodied in our care for God's children everywhere, by whatever means necessary. Prayer and protest go hand in hand.

Spirit, let my love for my grandchildren radiate to love for children everywhere. Let me hear their laughter and cry with their tears as I seek a world with liberty and justice for all.

# 74.

But let justice roll down like waters,
righteousness like an everflowing stream!

—AMOS 5:24

Amos was a shepherd and arborist before he was called to be a prophet, a speaker to the wealthy and powerful on behalf of God's vision of Shalom. When the "word of God" came to Amos in the eighth century before Jesus, God opened Amos's senses to the realities of farm foreclosures, neglect of the vulnerable, and the widening gap between the wealthy and poor. Amos had a secure life, he most likely was a parent, and possibly a grandparent. But he couldn't turn his back on God's mes-

sage to challenge the wealthy and powerful to do justice. Like most prophets, he didn't like the job description and would rather have stayed home.

The "word of God" comes to us on cable and network news and on our internet feeds. God's revelation comes through our discomfort when we see children separated from their parents on the US borderlands or witness the victims of police brutality. Few of us want to be prophets. We prefer watching the news to making it. But our love for our grandchildren reminds us that we must as a nation and as people change our ways. We must put justice and Earth care at the top of our agendas—and be models for our grandchildren, demonstrating a love that changes the world.

Spirit of Justice, help me feel Your presence in the daily news and discern how I might be a "prophet" of an alternative reality, the realm of justice.

# 75.

I should like a lake of the finest ale
for the King of Kings.
I should like a table of the choicest food
for the family of heaven. . . .
I should welcome the poor to my feast
for they are God's children.
I should welcome the sick to my feast
for they are God's joy.

—ST. BRIGID

Justice is about celebration. Celtic Saint Brigid imagines a smorgasbord of food and drink, welcoming the poor and vulnerable with all God's

children gathered around the groaning board, laughing and playing, rejoicing in bounty and making plans for a future without poverty and powerlessness.

These days, my grandchildren and I drop canned goods at church, and we are looking forward to shopping for Thanksgiving meals to share with others. They are learning the wisdom of Saint Brigid. Everyone belongs at the table. Everyone belongs in the front row. Everyone deserves healthy food. All children deserve celebration.

**Loving Spirit, help me to rejoice in the bounty of the Earth. Help me to remember that my largesse is for the welfare of others, not just my own pleasure. Let there be laughter and celebration around every table, for all are God's children.**

# 76.

Prayer changes the world as it is,
and therefore changes what the world can be.
Prayer opens the world to its own transformation.

## —MARJORIE SUCHOCKI

As a child, I encountered the refrigerator magnet, "Prayer changes things," whenever I opened the door to get a snack. Sixty years later, this maxim has new meaning for me. I don't believe that prayer is magic, forces God's hand, or is automatically answered. I do believe that when we pray, we inject new possibilities into the world. I believe that prayer can be a tipping point between hope and fear, life and death, and love and hate.

Every morning as I walk on the beach, I pray for my grandchildren as they prepare for school. I surround them with loving light that connects us throughout the day. I pray for wisdom in the conduct of my professional life and inspiration for my writing and teaching. I pray for political leaders and public policies. I pray for the right whale—there are only four hundred on the planet—entangled by a net off Cape Cod. While most of these prayers aren't immediately answered, I believe they make a difference. My prayers deepen my spiritual life, calm my mind, enable me to see holiness in challenging people, and inspire me to act. Prayer changes things, beginning with me and radiating out into the world, energetically and lovingly.

**Heart of the Universe, help me be attuned to Your movements in my life.**

# 77.

Picket and pray.

**—INSCRIPTION ON A BENCH
AT KIRKRIDGE RETREAT CENTER,
BANGOR, PENNYSLVANIA,
ATTRIBUTED TO JOHN OLIVER NELSON**

Contemplatives can be activists, and activists can be contemplative. Howard Thurman asserts that mysticism inspires us to social justice. Our encounters with God challenge us to confront any practice or policy that prevents people from experiencing abundant life. Injustice must be called out and resisted. Confrontation is necessary at times.

Still we must recognize the holiness of those we challenge. They too are God's children and their injustice may threaten their spiritual well-being. We can challenge with compassion. Protest and pray. Resist and reunite. Guided by our prayers, our preferential option for the poor and powerless will inspire us to seek the spiritual healing of those whom we oppose.

For our grandchildren's sake, let us picket and pray.

Let my prayers motivate protest. Let my contemplation provoke challenge. Let my hands, feet, and heart be dedicated to healing the soul of our nation and world. Even when I am no longer in this world, may my grandchildren be inspired by my example.

# 78.

Religion
is world loyalty.

## —ALFRED NORTH WHITEHEAD

Many people see faith as purely transactional. Their faith can be described as follows: "If I believe the right things or do the right things, then God will reward me with good fortune or salvation." Transactional faith is ultimately self-interested, centering on what God can do for us if we just get the right formula.

In contrast, I believe that a healthy and compassionate faith inspires us to widen our ethical interest from what benefits us personally to

what benefits our family and then to wider and wider circles of care. Deep spirituality goes from self-interest to world loyalty. Deep faith lives in the moment, rejoicing in this glorious day and its wonders, and then makes commitments to future generations, including generations we will never meet and communities we will never visit. World loyalty expands the scope of self-interest to include the well-being of others. We grow in wisdom and stature, becoming "fat souls," for whom the impact of our actions on the future are as important as our present happiness.

Soul of the Universe, expand my spirit to embrace the whole Earth and the generations of children and grandchildren. Let me rejoice in the now, knowing this moment well-lived brings beauty and health to future generations.

# 79.

In a life-centered ethic,
the first moral virtue is reverence for life . . .
an inward disposition that is
respectful of, and caring for
other animals, plants, and the Earth,
and refuses to draw a sharp dichotomy
between human life and other forms of life.

### —JAY MCDANIEL

These words from my Claremont Graduate University roommate Jay McDaniel alert us to the wondrous and intricate interdependence of life. While each human child is unique, humankind is

at the same time embedded in the Cosmic Adventure from the Big Bang to this moment. We are not aliens on the Earth, whose calling is dominion and destruction to serve our human ends. We are gardeners and siblings of all creation whose calling is to nurture and repair our planet.

The image of God unique to humankind, embracing the "he, she, and they" of creation, enables us to see the image of God in our grandchildren; we also see it nascent in the nonhuman world. Healthy spirituality takes us beyond the binary to embrace our common ancestry and common identity in God's Holy Adventure. Manifold, yet one, all creatures reflect their Creator.

**One in spirit with all creation, O Loving Creator, let me and the generations to come bless the Earth.**

# 80.

I was suddenly overwhelmed with the realization
that I loved all those people, that they
were mine and I was theirs, that we could
not be alien to one another even though
we were total strangers. It was like
waking from a dream of separateness.

## —THOMAS MERTON

Trappist monk and spiritual author Thomas Merton discovered that there is no "other." Each of us, though unique in experience and giftedness, are profoundly interdependent. In the fabric of relatedness, we are joined, and at

our depths the same Energy of Love and Wisdom flows through all of us. In a world of division, ICE agents and undocumented immigrants are one. Democrats and Republicans share the same human DNA and Divine origins. The Black Lives Matter protester and the anxious white nationalist both bleed red.

As Oscar Hammerstein writes, "You've got to be taught to hate and fear." Let us teach our grandchildren kinship with all life. May they rejoice in diversity and multiple paths to God and give thanks for the ties that bind us all.

**Spirit of Graceful Interdependence, blessed be the ties that bind. Blessed be the colors and voices of life. Blessed be the cultures and ethnicities. Blessed be the exceptional and the commonplace. Blessed be!**

# 81.

Our calling
is to do something beautiful
for God.

## —MOTHER TERESA

When we walk in beauty we never walk alone. When we commit ourselves to sharing beauty, we are joined with every creature. While life is multifaceted and takes us beyond the binary, in the broadest sense, we have two contrasting choices: Will we add to the beauty of the Earth? Or will we add to the ugliness of the Earth? Will we promote unity and respect or

division and incivility? In other words, will we give God a beautiful world or an ugly one? This is the choice we make moment by moment.

The choices we make are as simple as smiling across the room at a life partner. Helping a grandchild struggle with a math assignment. Responding to a quarrel between siblings. Encountering a stranger, unkempt and troubled, and seeing Christ in disguise. With beauty all around us, we walk. With beauty flowing from us, we act, making our lives our gift to the One Who Covers Earth with Beauty.

O Beautiful Spirit, let me know my beauty, and out of that realization, let me be a beauty-giver, doing something beautiful for You moment by moment and day by day. May I see You in my grandchildren's faces.

# 82.

Tell me, Father, why is there so much
pain and darkness in my soul?
Sometimes I find myself saying,
"I can't bear it any longer"
and with the same breath I say,
"I'm sorry. Do with me what you wish."

## —MOTHER TERESA

Many people were shocked to discover that despite her saintliness, Mother Teresa experienced spiritual and emotional depression for many decades. After her ecstatic experience of God's voice guiding her to a new vocation, she was plunged into the dark night of the soul,

often doubting her calling and God's love for her. Although she felt great inner emptiness, she continued to greet the lost and forgotten of the world with a smile. She walked forward one step at a time, giving Christ to "the least of these," while seeing Christ in others, despite her sense of Christ's absence in her own life.

As every parent, grandparent, and faithful spouse and friend understands, love is about commitment, not how we are feeling at any given moment. Even in the darkness we can dedicate our lives to our grandchildren and to our fellow sufferers, seeing the Christ in them and rediscovering it in ourselves.

**In deep darkness, Spirit, give us light for the journey. Let the light take us beyond our self-concern to care for others.**

# 83.

I was that mother whose child
had been raped and slain.
I was the mother who had borne
the monster who had done it.
I was even that monster who had done it. . . .
I was the oppressed. I was that drug addict,
screaming and tossing in her cell,
beating her head against the wall.

**—DOROTHY DAY**

World loyalty is the gift of mystic unity. World loyalty emerges when we see all persons as pilgrims and no person as a stranger. When we

truly go beyond our privilege and defensiveness to feel the joy and pain of others. When we feel the suffocation of George Floyd in our own shortness of breath. When we call out to our mama, gasping for one more breath. When we feel the defensiveness and fear of a white nationalist. When we feel the hopelessness of a mother in a Syrian refugee camp and the anger of protesters calling out, "Say her name!" Their interest is our interest. Their struggle is our struggle.

As grandparents, we expand our spirits to feel our grandchildren's anxiety about the pandemic, worry about failure, and emotional highs and lows. As barriers break down, our love for our grandchildren joins us with all children and our loyalty to nation becomes world loyalty.

**Spirit who breathes through all creation, let me feel the joy and pain of my siblings.**

# 84.

I am the twelve-year-old girl, refugee on a
small boat, who throws herself into the ocean
after being raped by a sea pirate. And I am also
the pirate, my heart not yet capable of seeing and loving. . . . Please call me by my true
names, so I can hear all my cries and laughter
at once, so I can see that my joy and pain are
one. Please call me by my true names,
so I can wake up and the door of my heart
could be left open, the door of compassion.

**—THICH NHAT HANH**

When Thomas Merton and Thich Naht Hanh
met, the Trappist and Buddhist monks saw

in the other a kindred spirit. Thich Nhat Hanh noted, "This was the first time that I had been struck by such a feeling of spirituality in anyone who professed Christianity." Both knew that there is no "other." We are all reflections of each other.

Despite our age differences, our grandchildren are reflections of us and we reflect them. Our joys and sorrows are one. We teach them and then become their students. We model goodness for them and then learn generosity from them. Our hearts beat as one, beneath the surface. Our grandchildren inspire us to open our hearts, to throw wide open the doors of compassion, to laugh and cry together, play and pray together, and let our joy and pain go forth into an ever-expanding spiral of lovingkindness.

**O Loving Parent, let me see You in each face. Let me know myself in each embrace.**

# 85.

Humanity's legacy of stories and storytelling
is the most precious we have.
All wisdom is in our stories and songs.
A story is how we construct our experiences.

## —DORIS LESSING

Storytelling is liberating for those whose voices have been silenced due to race, class, politics, gender, age (both youths and elders), and sexuality. Stories are often told by the "winners," the celebrity, mogul, and politician. But everyone has a story.

During the time of pandemic, I began writing an informal memoir for my grandchildren. With-

out being morbid, I realized that my age put me at greater risk than younger persons. I wanted to give witness to the pivotal experiences of my life, my growing up, and my faith and values. I wanted to leave a written document to accompany the love I have for them. I wanted to leave a testimony beyond my lifespan.

It has been said that God created humans because God loves stories. Your story can be a window into the universe, an account of a heroic journey and reminder that in the twenty-first century, you walked upon this good Earth and in the walking, changed the world.

Loving Spirit, remind me that my life is valuable—that my story matters and that in sharing my story with future generations, I will find my own voice and invite them to voice their lives, out loud and lovingly.

# 86.

Love is something if you give it away,
you end up having more.

**—MALVINA REYNOLDS**

Over fifty years ago, I sat in my friend Paula's living room, and was introduced to the music of folk singer Malvina Reynolds. A high school senior at the time, I was just learning the meaning of love—and now nearly seventy, I am still learning to deepen my love for my family, congregants, and friends. One thing I have learned as a husband of over forty years as well as a father, grandfather, and friend, is that love is expansive.

The more we share, the more we always get back. Grounded in God's Energy of Love, our human loves share in eternity and are constantly replenished by the Loving Heart of the Universe.

So, give your love. Let it flow to your grandchildren and out into the world. Don't hoard your heart, for when you give it away, you end up having more.

Dear Heart of the Universe beating in every heart, beat strong in my heart, so that I may love my grandchildren—and the rest of the world—more deeply, generously, and faithfully.

# 87.

Be a good ancestor.
Stand for something bigger than yourself.
Add value to the Earth during your sojourn.

## —MARIAN WRIGHT EDELMAN

Children's advocate and founder of the Children's Defense Fund, Marian Wright Edelman reminds us that we are part of an intricate fabric of life. We all stand on the shoulders and share the wisdom of those who have gone before us.

None of us is self-made. All of us are a creative synthesis of our life experiences, including the gifts of our parents and grandparents. Now that I am a grandparent, I must consciously choose

to be a good ancestor to my two grandchildren, sharing my love and values, my time and energy. Being a good ancestor, though, means more than loving my own grandchildren. As an elder, my responsibility is to look seven generations beyond my own lifespan. It also means being involved in confronting climate change, racism, homophobia, economic injustice, and gender inequality. It means loving other people's grandchildren—even those I'll never meet—with the same good will that I love my own. I want to be a good ancestor. To leave beauty beyond myself. To provide opportunities for the next generation's spiritual journey. To bring hope beyond my lifetime by choosing life for the planet as well as my family.

**Holy One, may my days on this good Earth be filled with beauty. Give me a heart and hands to serve generations to come.**

# 88.

I came that they may have life,
and have it abundantly.

—JOHN 10:10

Over forty years ago as a graduate student, I heard one of my professors, David Ray Griffin, assert that "God wants us to enjoy. God wants all of us to enjoy." Professor Griffin meant something more than hedonism. He meant enjoying the gift of life and sharing of life's bounties and beauties to bring joy to all humanity. Abundant life was at the heart of Jesus' mission statement. God's aim at Shalom, at wholeness and abundance, is for

everyone and involves everyone's commitments. God can't do it alone. To paraphrase Teresa of Avila, we are God's hands and feet, and in following Jesus' path, we can affirm that we too came into this world that all might have abundant life. Generosity of spirit, time, talent, and treasure expands the Energy of Love flowing through our lives and into our grandchildren's. It enables us to share more and enjoy more of life's blessings.

Be abundant in living and giving, rejoicing in the birth of each new child and your role in bringing beauty to this good Earth.

Let me share in Your abundance with my grandchildren, Spirit of All Good Gifts, letting Your love funnel through me to bless them and everyone I meet.

# 89.

In the time of your life, live—so that in that
good time there shall be no ugliness or death
for yourself or for any life your life touches. Seek
goodness everywhere, and when it is found, bring
it out of its hiding place and let it be free and
unashamed. . . . In the time of your life, live—so
that in that wondrous time you shall not add to
the misery and sorrow of the world, but shall
smile to the infinite delight and mystery of it.

**—WILLIAM SAROYAN**

Our lives, well-lived, are our legacy to our
grandchildren and to the future generations

that come after them. Love endures forever. Nothing loved is lost but lives on in God's memory and in the memories and the spiritual DNA of those who follow us. In being "love finders," to quote attitudinal healing pioneer Jerry Jampolsky, we smile to the infinite delight and mystery of life and impart that delight and openness to adventure to our grandchildren and those placed in our lives.

Let your life speak each day by acts of kindness and love. Let your love, values, and compassion be a legacy that adds to the beauty and goodness of the world. Living each moment fully, your love lasts forever.

**In the time of my life, Spirit, let me live fully and abundantly, with compassion and passion. Let each day be an opportunity to share my gift and be my legacy to generations to come.**

# 90.

What we do or don't do now,
will affect my entire generation,
and the lives of my children and grandchildren.

### —GRETA THUNBERG

What will your legacy be? What will you answer when your grandchildren ask, "What did you do when George Floyd was killed by law enforcement officers? Did Black Lives Matter to you? What did you do about climate change? Did you show up or stand on the sidelines as our futures slipped away?"

Each one of us can make a difference. Our decisions radiate out into the universe, shaping our families, communities, and planet. We love our grandchildren and they know it, but how will our action or inaction shape the world in which they will grow up? Will we be happy about the world they will inherit from us? Will we make plans to ensure a better world for their children? Life is questioning us. Their future selves and unborn children are beckoning to us. God is questioning us. Generations to come need us to be good ancestors.

Loving Spirit, You have given us a vision of the future—the ways of life and the ways of death. Help us to choose life for ourselves and our grandchildren. Let us be responsible ancestors for the generations to come.

# 91.

The worship of God is not a rule of safety—
it is an adventure of the spirit,
the flight after the unattainable.
The death of religion comes with the repression
of the high hope of adventure.

## —ALFRED NORTH WHITEHEAD

God calls us to be part of a holy adventure. The future is not predestined nor are we imprisoned by our past decisions. Each day brings something new into the world and our lives. As the author of Lamentations notes, "God's mercies are new every morning." This day invites us—in

obvious and subtle ways—to be God's companions in a spiritual adventure that will radiate beyond our lifetimes, into our grandchildren's lifetimes and beyond.

In this day, we can save a child, speak out for justice, plant seeds of healing, and bring beauty to this good Earth. Adventure awaits. We may have to push beyond our comfort zones. We may have to confront xenophobia and bullying and look hard at our own prejudice. We may have to change our habits and examine our values. The future is not safe, but as we venture forth, trusting God's holy adventure, each day will be filled with beauty, wonder, love, and companionship with the Great Adventurer we call God.

**Adventurous Spirit, guide our steps toward the future. Use our hands, hearts, minds, and feet to chart frontiers of wholeness and love.**

# 92.

Love is patient; love is kind;
love is not envious or boastful
or arrogant or rude.
It does not insist on its own way;
it is not irritable or resentful;
it does not rejoice in wrong-doing,
but rejoices in the truth.
It bears all things, believes all things,
hopes all things, endures all things.

—I CORINTHIANS 12:4–7

The early Christian teacher, Paul of Tarsus, describes the virtues of love and sees our lives as a laboratory for loving. Many of us have

discovered that while falling in love is easy, and often unintentional, staying in love is hard work, requiring a day-to-day commitment to embrace our highest self as we let our love flow to others. In the end, a good life involves the integration of faith, hope, and love, but the greatest is love.

Love involves embracing the holy otherness of our families and friends. Our children and grandchildren are unique and differ from us in personality and life experience. While this may lead to tension, love accepts and affirms differences, seeking to bring out the best in those whom we love. Not bound by the present moment but leaning toward eternity, "love bears all things, believes all things, hopes all things, endures all things. Love never ends."

**Loving and graceful Spirit, let my love take me beyond self-interest to care for my grandchildren and others.**

# 93.

You shall love the Lord your God
with all your heart, and with all your soul
and with all your mind,
and with all your strength. . . .
You shall love your neighbor as yourself.
There is no other commandment
greater than these.

—MARK 12:30-31

Healthy loving relationships integrate our love of God, neighbor, and ourselves, grounded in our experience of the dynamic unity of life. "Love yourself," Jesus counsels. Honor who you are.

Affirm your gifts. Develop your gifts for service so that your joy adds to the joy of the world. Let your self-affirmation take shape in affirming others, including your grandchildren, promoting their authentic well-being along with your own.

Love is personal and political. When we love, we promote others' well-being and work so that they have the same advantages that we have. Love expands the spirit and deep love delights in the unique spirits of others, and we serve our grandchildren by modeling those values.

Spirit, let my self-affirmation lead to affirming the unique gifts of others. Let our individuality be part of the great and wondrous symphony of life.

# 94.

Love does not consist of gazing at each other,
but in looking outward together
in the same direction.

## —ANTOINE DE SAINT-EXUPÉRY

A love that grows our spirits and expands our sense of mission looks toward the far horizon as well as in each other's eyes. Loving relationships are grounded in a sense of shared values and purposes. They don't end with a couple's intimacy but expand to embrace the world. While romance may need to be rekindled, loving relationships look forward toward new adventures.

With over forty years of marriage behind me, I have come to appreciate the words of Robert Browning: "Grow old along with me! The best is yet to be, the last of life, for which the first was made." Children and grandchildren redefine the nature of love. Our love becomes more selfless and oriented toward projects whose fruits we may never harvest. Though we rejoice in this day that God has made, our love inspires us to be loving ancestors who sacrifice, so that the new generations experience the beauty of a healthy planet, equality of opportunity, and unhindered imaginations. New projects await and friends and lovers embrace the seeds of the future embedded in the Holy Here and Now.

Let my love be visionary, Spirit, delighting in the moment yet guided by far horizons of hope. Let my love be generative, planting seeds of possibility for generations I will not see.

# 95.

If hating is the worst way to exert your energy,
love is the best way to use your energy.
The more you give, the more you get.
Be compassionate.
Tell those you love that you love them.

## —MALALA YOUSAFZAI

The victim of violence herself, Malala challenges us to go beyond hate to embrace love so that we can reconcile enemies and create community amid great diversity. It has been said that the opposite of love is fear. Fear is the foundation of hate that we see in religious fundamentalists, white supremacists, and abusive partners.

Falling into fear and hate spirals us into future violence.

One of the greatest gifts we can give our grandchildren is our modeling of peaceful conflict resolution revealed in our civility and respect for those with whom we differ. We model God's love in our ability to protest injustice without hating the perpetrators of injustice. Even the oppressor is carrying a great burden—the cumbersome weight of hate, fear, and anxiety in the face of a changing world. Love alone can heal our social incivility and divisiveness. Love alone, spoken and acted out, is the only hope for our nation and the energy that nurtures the spirits of future generations.

Spirit of Lovingkindness, teach me to love in words and deeds. Teach me how to prayerfully protest injustice and be examples of reconciliation in my family and community. My grandchildren are watching.

# 96.

Fame is fun, money is useful, celebrity can be exciting, but finally life is about optimal well-being and how we achieve that in a dominator culture, in a greedy culture, in a culture that uses so much of the world's resources. How do men and women, boys and girls, live lives of compassion, justice and love . . . that's the visionary challenge for feminism and all other progressive movements for social change.

**—BELL HOOKS**

How do boys and girls, our grandchildren, live lives of compassion, justice, and love? That is the question that inspires our everyday acts of

nurture and sacrifice. Words of love matter, and you can't spoil a child by saying "I love you" too many times throughout the day. Along with words of love is love in action: everyday kindnesses and consideration that tell children that they matter, that what they say is important, that their feelings count, and that you stand by them regardless of what the future brings.

Raising girls to be bold and courageous, to be leaders, takes grandparents who affirm "yes, you can" and spend time supporting their giftedness. Raising boys to respect women and promote equality in the various gender and sexual expression takes grandparents who affirm equality and value regardless of sexuality, gender, and race.

Loving One, let me speak only love and act with kindness joined with justice toward humanity in all its diverse and amazing expressions.

# 97.

No one has greater love than this,
to lay down one's life
or one's friends.

**—JOHN 15:13**

For several years, I was a volunteer tutor at our grandson's elementary school. It was a joy to be part of children's intellectual and—dare I say—spiritual growth by my affirmative approach to education. Yet, after the Parkland school shootings, I experienced a sea change in my approach to tutoring. When I entered the school, I looked for threats. I even planned out what I would do if an active shooter entered the school building.

I can't claim to be brave but I knew that my love for the children required me to protect them from any dangers, even if it meant sacrificing my life.

Great love requires the possibility of sacrifice. Trusting as Jesus did in the deep and eternal love of God, we can let go of property and possessions and even safety and security to ensure the well-being of vulnerable children and adults. The time of our lives and our lives themselves are our gifts to our grandchildren and children everywhere. Let us be protectors and caretakers, gardeners and shepherds, trusting our lives to God and willing to let go of life itself to save the lives of others.

Grant us wisdom and courage, Spirit, for facing the challenges of today. Let us be lovingly bold and sacrificially strong, to be peacekeepers and life givers, whatever the cost.

# 98.

Love is or it ain't.
Thin love ain't love at all.

## —TONI MORRISON

As Toni Morrison says in *Beloved*, there is no thin love. The love we need—and the love we need to give—must be thick in commitment and compassion. I always counsel couples to make maximal vows in their marriage. While they may not choose traditional words like "for better or for worse, for richer or for poorer, in sickness and in health," strong vows remind us that we must be prepared

to love in a future that is unknown to us. The same applies to parenting and grandparenting, neither of which is for the wishy-washy or fainthearted.

Perhaps, we should make explicit grandparenting vows to embrace all the joyful and tragic contingencies of life, to remind us that grandparenting is a vocation, an act of commitment, to the greater good of our grandchildren and the world they grow up in. Let us, with Toni Morrison, have thick and strong loves, protective and challenging, accepting and affirming, facing both light and darkness with commitment, and enduring in companionship and hope forever.

Holy One, let my love be strong and faithful, affirming life and facing death, never giving up and always nurturing.

# 99.

In the midst of life,
we are surrounded by death.
In the midst of death,
we are surrounded by life.

### —MARTIN LUTHER

Most of us become grandparents in midlife. When our first grandchild was born, I was 57 years old. I often quipped, "I am in midlife, provided I live to be 114." Ten years have passed, and my comments have a touch of gallows humor, since to claim midlife now I must live to be 136.

As we age, we become more and more aware that we are surrounded by death.

We are also surrounded by life. The forces of Divine energy enliven, inspire, and challenges us to embrace each day and God's everlasting adventure. My daily prayer is to trust God in life and death, so that I might live courageously and lovingly. How we face death is our gift to our grandchildren. As they observe our positive responses to mortality, they will learn practices of compassion, courage, and commitment. They will discover eternity in the midst of time.

**Spirit of Life and Death and Eternity, give us courage to face our mortality. Give us wisdom to choose life in the midst of death. Give us love for those who are suffering and solidarity with those who grieve.**

# 100.

For I am convinced that neither death, nor life,
nor angels, nor rulers, nor things present,
nor things to come, nor powers, nor height,
nor depth, nor anything else in all creation,
will be able to separate us
from the love of God in Christ Jesus our Lord.

—ROMANS 8:38-39

What is your deepest fear? What wakes you up in a cold sweat at 3:00 a.m. or haunts your days? As grandparents, we are forced to accept that our deaths lie ahead; we can no longer pretend we will live forever. Life is risky business; no

one gets out alive. This is especially true when we find ourselves increasingly vulnerable due to age and health factors.

But nothing can overwhelm God's love. No threat can separate us from God. No fear can nullify God's love. No death can stand in the way of God's everlasting life. The One who loved us into life will greet us with loving arms at the hour of our death. Truly nothing can separate us from the love of God.

Loving Spirit, we know that our mortality can paralyze us, but it can also expand our compassion. Move within our anxieties to give us confidence in Your unending grace. Give us faith for today and bright hopes for tomorrow. May our grandchildren see in us our faith in You, our joy in life, and our courage to face death.

# 101.

There is a land of the living
and a land of the dead
and the bridge is love,
the only survival, the only meaning.

## –THORNTON WILDER

In the Apostle Paul's Corinthian hymn to love, he proclaims that "love never ends." Whatever is loved shares in eternity. Whatever is cherished outlives the grave. There is a bridge—a thin place—that joins time and eternity and this lifetime and our destiny in God's everlasting realm. The everlasting God touches each moment as it arises and perishes and ensures that nothing of beauty is lost. No love is forgotten.

Earth and heaven are interdependent. In the wondrous transparency of Life Everlasting, we may touch our deceased relatives and the communion of saints touches us. One of my friends reports that she often receives a sense of love and guidance from her grandmother. Another receives messages from a deceased spiritual friend. While I am a rationalist, philosophically from the "show me" state of Missouri, I too have felt the presence and guidance of friends from beyond the grave. Love is the bridge.

Who knows? We may be able to share subtle energies of love with our grandchildren, from beyond the grave. The love we have for each other will not end. The love that birthed creation invites us to holy adventures beyond the grave.

**Open me, Spirit, to love that joins the living and the deceased. Open me to wisdom from the saints and ancestors.**

# About the Author

The grandparent of two elementary school boys, with whom he learns and plays daily, Bruce Epperly is a Cape Cod pastor, professor, and author of over 50 books, including *Become Fire: Guideposts for Postmodern Pilgrims*, *Spirit Online: A Mystic's Guide to the Internet*, *Thin Places Everywhere: The 12 Days of Christmas with Celtic Christianity*, and *Piglet's Process: Process Theology for All God's Children*.

# 101 Soul Seeds

## for Parents of Adult Children

Being a parent held joys and challenges every step of the way, and never more so than when our children finally made it to adulthood. Now we can connect with them on deeper levels than ever—but unexpected potential pitfalls dot this new path we're traveling. *101 Soul Seeds for Parents of Adult Children* offers observations and quotes, coupled with simple prayers to help us navigate this por-

tion of parenting . . . so we and our adult children grow closer to one another and closer to our own souls' destination.

**Paperback Price: $12.99**

**Kindle Price: $4.99**

# 101 Soul Seeds

## for Coping with a Covid Christmas

*101 Soul Seeds for Coping with a Covid Christmas* ministers to both body and soul during this singularly difficult and constraining time in recent human history. It offers practical suggestions to create a satisfying holiday experience despite the Covid-19 pandemic, along with deeper thoughts on the spiritual significance of everything we do.

**Paperback Price: $12.99**

**Kindle Price: $4.99**

# AℕAᴍⒸHARA
## BOOKS

www.AnamcharaBooks.com

Made in the USA
Middletown, DE
02 September 2021